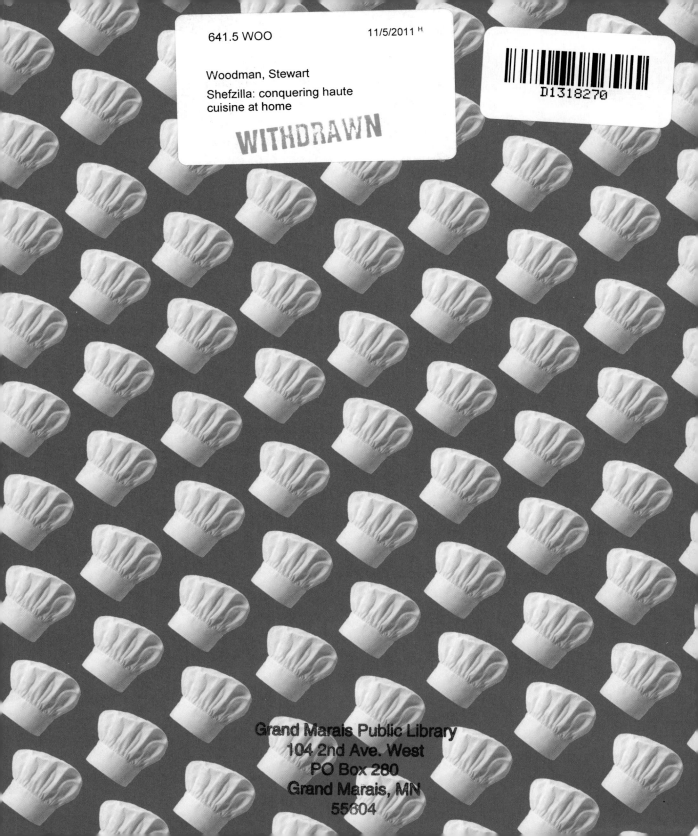

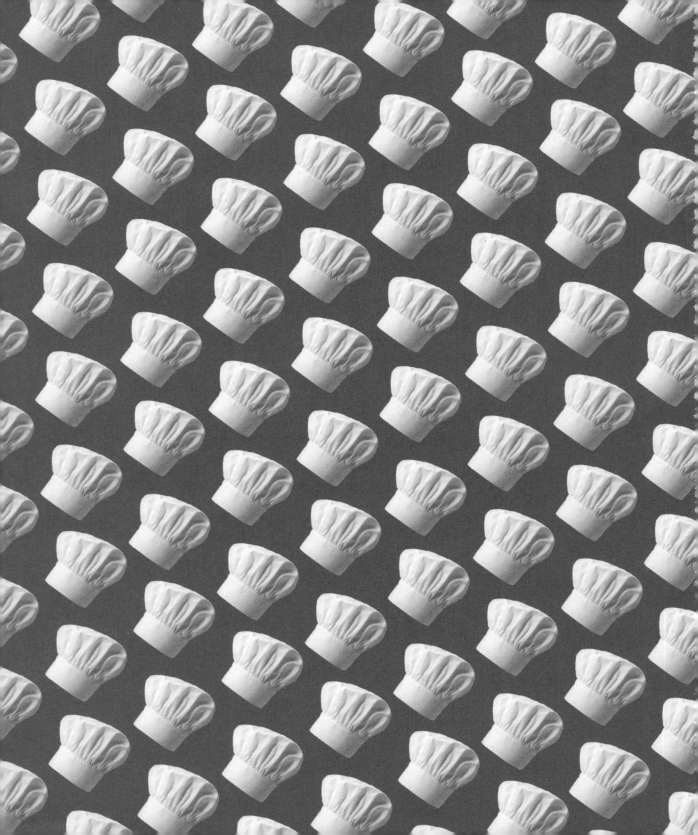

STEWART WOODMAN

SHEFZILLA

CONQUERING HAUTE CUISINE AT HOME

STEWART WOODMAN

SHEFZILLA

CONQUERING HAUTE CUISINE AT HOME

BOREALIS BOOKS

Borealis Books is an imprint of the Minnesota Historical Society Press.

www.borealisbooks.org

The Minnesota Historical Society Press is a member of the Association of American University Presses.

Manufactured in Canada

10 9 8 7 6 5 4 3 2 1

∞ The paper used in this publication meets the minimum requirements of the American National Standard for Information Sciences — Permanence for Printed Library Materials, ANSI Z39.48–1984.

International Standard Book Number
ISBN: 978-0-87351-809-3 (cloth)

Library of Congress Cataloging-in-Publication Data

Woodman, Stewart.
    Shefzilla : conquering haute cuisine at home / Stewart Woodman.
        p.   cm.
    Includes index.
    ISBN 978-0-87351-809-3 (cloth : alk. paper)
    1. Cookery.   I. Title.
    TX714.W6635   2010
    614.5 — dc22   2010023348

Shefzilla is set using the typeface Cronos, with the font Blackoak for the display. It was designed by Jim Davis of Mind*Spark Creative, northeast Minneapolis. Typesetting and composition by Allan Johnson of Phoenix Type, Appleton, Minnesota.

CONTENTS

For Heidi, who alone has helped me fulfill
my dreams and aspirations.

For my sons, Isaac and Aaron, without whom
this book would not have been
nearly as much fun to write.

And for David and Vicky:
thank you for the DNA and for
teaching me to have the
courage to follow my bliss.

STEWART WOODMAN

SHEFZILLA

CONQUERING HAUTE CUISINE AT HOME

INTRODUCTION

In February 2010, on a sunny Thursday afternoon, a fire broke out in the kitchen of my restaurant, Heidi's Minneapolis. By the time it was extinguished, the building was destroyed. When I came up for air a couple of weeks later, I knew in my heart we could not go back. A restaurant is more than the food and the service; the feelings and spirit of the place could never be rebuilt in exactly the same way. I also knew that we had poured so much love into creating an extraordinary dining experience through the atmosphere, the service, and the food that we would need to capture some part of it — if only the food — to buoy our spirits.

We set out at a feverish pace to re-create, in my home kitchen, some of the magic that was Heidi's Minneapolis.

As a pro in the restaurant business, I had not cooked at home much — perhaps on three dozen occasions over twenty years. Most of my time was spent in restaurant kitchens, of course; plus my wife, Heidi, is also a professional cook and a fabulous one to boot. When I sit down to a meal she has prepared for the family, it is as if I have never eaten. To me, the idea of cooking at home seemed so much more laborious: the fumbling with a stuffed fridge, the perpetual sink full of dishes.

My career at that point spanned more than two decades. Most of it had been spent working in the best kitchens I could find. I had become a journeyman in the classic sense of the term, especially in the New York years, when I spent significant time in each kitchen and then moved on to the next challenge or answered the call to take on a new role elsewhere. By the time I left town, I had worked as a sous-chef for Eric Ripert, Jean-Georges Vongerichten, and Alain Ducasse. I had also worked in the kitchens of the mightily talented Gray Kunz and Michael Romano. Briefly, I had even

been an executive chef, from summer through Thanksgiving 2001, at a restaurant located unfortunately close to Ground Zero, whose owners had to lay off much of its staff, myself included. We surveyed the landscape and, with the arrival of our first baby only weeks away, decided to make a break for it, to pursue the dream of having it all—the successful cooking career and a happy, healthy family life.

We packed up a U-Haul and made our way to Minneapolis, Heidi's hometown. So often this part of the Midwest is labeled "fly-over country," but these days I can't help but feel a twinge of pity for those who discount the region outright, who will never be open to hearing a hearty "you betcha" or feeling a sweet prairie breeze blowing across their face. Immediately comfortable, we made short work of settling in and within about a year opened a four-star restaurant. I could, I suppose, attribute this feat to our team's talents, but the reality is that we were welcomed with open arms—even the goofiest of experiments was embraced. Within a few years and with some dear friends, we opened Heidi's, finally a restaurant that we ourselves owned.

After the fire, we could no longer look to what had been; we had to deal with what was—and that meant nowhere for me to cook. I was invited into our home kitchen, and I took it over. (I'm sure Heidi much preferred me busy chopping and stirring than spending time in the living room doing squats to Billy Blanks.) First I had to think in terms of making something for four people instead of the usual twenty-five. I had to relearn how to cook in a strange new landscape with different tools and wimpy burners. In truth, I had regarded the appliances and utensils available to the home cook with disdain, even as beneath me.

Once I figured out where the salt was kept and how to keep from knocking the kids' magnets off the fridge, things began to take shape. Then something happened that I didn't expect and still find utterly baffling: suddenly, I fell in love with cooking all over again. It turns out that cooking at home is a joy, one I had somehow forgotten. I found myself remembering that as a child I had avidly watched my mother cook, that the first book I bought was a cookbook, that making the ideal peanut butter cookie was an early passion, that I had dreamt about preparing the perfect meal for my family, one that would silence my siblings' harsh criticisms.

Working in a professional kitchen, with its constant whir and din, the über-focus on perfection, can stifle the intimate experience that comes with preparing something in your home. Subtleties can be missed. At home, as I stirred bubbling pots, I heard sparrows playing in the bush by the back window, dogs barking, and lawn mowers buzzing in the neighborhood. Soon we asked friends to test the recipes in their homes, and the excitement started to build as they told us how the flavors of the dishes reminded them of meals with us at the restaurant.

I cooked for my wife and kids for the first time in my life. Sure, I'd pulled together a couple of meals here and there, but nowhere near daily. As I re-created recipes I had used as a chef, the results became a new chapter in our family's food life. Adapted for home use meant recipes needed to be singular, uncomplicated. I felt inclined to cook in a more meaningful and less showy way, so that, for example, the casings came off the chicken sausages and they became patties. These, I'll have you know, are now a highly sought-after meal.

Setting out to write this book amid a sad time, I received a great gift. If you grasp even an inkling of how much fun I had in remaking these dishes — and discover a similar joy in your own kitchen — it will all have been worthwhile. Bon appétit.

While assembling this book, I didn't frequent the usual restaurant supply spots. I asked myself with every dish if it would be too much of a bear to secure what folks would need at home. It's not a restaurant cookbook filled with hard-to-find ingredients and difficult or impossible to purchase one-off equipment. Having said that, I would like to introduce you to my little friends, the necessities, sometimes obscure but oh so worthwhile:

Whole spices: my favorites are obvious — coriander seed, cumin, star anise, pink peppercorns; see instructions on page 153 for toasting

Truffles! — salt, oil, and puree

Coconut milk

Sriracha — the red rooster

Fish sauce: Three Crabs brand

Spring roll wrappers

Kimchi

Sake, brandy, red and white wine: for cooking, don't waste your dough on these

High-quality extra-virgin olive oil: definitely waste your dough on this

Fermented black beans

Vinegar, especially rice wine and sherry

Beluga lentils, the little black ones

Sesame seeds, white and black

Phyllo dough

Grana Padano

Mustard seed oil: use sparingly — a little goes a long way

Exotic spices like long peppercorns and saffron

Kosher salt: salt without the additives, guaranteed

Finishing salts like fleur de sel

Fresh herbs: cilantro, mint, and thyme get you places and make for fabulous oils if they start to sit for more than a few days

Nutella, a personal weakness

APPETIZERS

BUFFALO SHRIMP SKEWERS

MAKES 26–30 PIECES

These all-in-one buffalo shrimp are party friendly, requiring no dips or extra condiments.

BLUE CHEESE SAUCE

2 tablespoons butter

2 tablespoons flour

1 cup skim milk

¾ teaspoon salt

2 ounces blue cheese

1. Melt butter over medium heat in a medium (2-quart) saucepan. Add flour and cook 2 minutes, stirring constantly with a wooden spoon.

2. Add milk and salt. Turn heat to high and stir constantly while bringing mixture to a boil. Reduce heat to medium and simmer 8 to 10 minutes, stirring occasionally to prevent burning.

3. Reduce heat to low; add cheese and stir 30 seconds. Remove from heat. Cool sauce to room temperature.

TO PREPARE SHRIMP AND SERVE:

1 pound large (26/30) shrimp, peeled and deveined

4- to 6-inch bamboo skewers, soaked in cold water

1. Get your grill on. Hold shrimp straight and push skewer through tail toward head. Repeat with remaining shrimp and skewers, one shrimp per skewer. Refrigerate skewered shrimp until grill is ready.

2. Grill shrimp over high heat, 1 to 2 minutes per side. Remove from heat and allow shrimp to cool slightly.

3. Dip each skewered shrimp into blue cheese sauce to coat thinly. Roll shrimp in Panko Crust, and serve immediately.

FOR PANKO CRUST:

3 tablespoons butter

½ cup panko (Japanese bread crumbs)

½ teaspoon cayenne pepper

¼ teaspoon salt

1. Heat large sauté pan over medium heat. Melt butter and add panko, cayenne, and salt.

2. Cook mixture over medium heat, stirring frequently, until golden brown, about 10 minutes. Remove from heat. Drain toasted bread crumbs on a paper towel; set aside.

Buffalo Shrimp Skewers

CARAMELIZED ONION BEEF SAUCE

1 tablespoon canola oil

2 medium onions, sliced

½ teaspoon salt

1 cup white wine

3 cups Beef Stock (p. 163)

1 sprig thyme

1. Heat sauté pan over high heat; add oil. When oil is hot, add onions and salt. Reduce heat to medium and cook 40 minutes, stirring occasionally.

2. Add wine; reduce almost entirely. Add Beef Stock and thyme; reduce by two-thirds. Remove from heat.

YUKON GOLD POUTINE

SERVES 4

Having grown up in Montreal, I reserve a special place in my heart for poutine. Give me fries with gooey cheese and meat stock any day of the week — twice after hockey practice.

FOR POTATOES:
4 medium Yukon Gold potatoes
2 cups canola oil

1. Rinse potatoes well and dry. Do not peel. Cut lengthwise into ½-inch-wide batons.

2. Heat oil to 225°F in a large saucepan; cook potato batons 10 minutes, until tender. Remove batons from oil using a slotted spoon, and cool completely on a plate. Set aside potatoes and reserve oil.

TO ASSEMBLE AND SERVE:
¼ cup fontina cheese, grated on a microplane

1. Preheat oven to 450°F. Heat sauté pan containing 1 inch of reserved oil until smoking.

2. Add potato pieces and pan fry until golden brown, 3 minutes. Remove potato to paper towel–lined plate; sprinkle with salt.

3. Divide potatoes among 4 oven-safe dishes, stacking like Lincoln Logs. Pour Caramelized Onion Beef Sauce evenly over potatoes. Sprinkle with cheese.

4. Bake about 5 minutes, until cheese is melted. Serve immediately.

Yukon Gold Poutine

JUMBO CRAB "NACHOS"

"Crab Nachos," the reservation would read, and we knew that Carolyn and Kai would be coming in and they hoped to be served this dish from the opening menu. Toward the end, others requested it as well and we had a sleeper on our hands: an "off-menu" menu item.

Jumbo Crab "Nachos"

FOR RICE PUFFS:
2 cups canola oil
1 package 8-inch spring roll wrappers

1. Heat canola oil to 375°F in a large sauté pan on high heat. Place 1 spring roll sheet in hot oil using tongs and push wrapper into the oil as sheet puffs.

2. When sheet is done cooking, 5 to 10 seconds, remove from oil and place on paper towel–lined plate. Repeat with remaining sheets. Sprinkle sheets with a pinch of salt. Set aside.

FOR CRAB SALAD:
1 pound jumbo lump crab meat
3 teaspoons minced chives (reserve tips for garnish)
⅛ teaspoon cayenne pepper
4 tablespoons Mayonnaise (p. 169)
¼ teaspoon salt
1 teaspoon sesame oil
2 tablespoons rice wine vinegar

Pick through crab meat and remove any shells. Squeeze crab meat dry by hand and place in medium mixing bowl. Add remaining ingredients (chives through vinegar) and mix well.

PRESENTATION:
½ cup Cilantro Pesto (p. 150)
2 tablespoons crushed pink peppercorns

Break puffed rice paper into pieces about 2 to 3 inches in diameter and arrange on plate or tray. Spoon 1 teaspoon Cilantro Pesto and about 1 tablespoon crab salad onto each piece of puffed rice paper. Top crab salad with a chive tip. Sprinkle with crushed pink peppercorns. Serve immediately.

Gray Kunz was the first chef to go out of his way for me, opening the door at Le Bernardin by calling Eric Ripert and asking him to consider me for a position. When Kunz called to tell me to visit with Ripert, I stood in Times Square thinking I had no way to repay that debt.

Years later, after I had been let go from my chef position, before we made the decision to leave New York, Kunz and I met for coffee a few times. I asked him about leaving—if I could return one day. "No," he said. "This place is so self-obsessed that once you go you can't come back. This world will have moved on, and you will be forsaken.

"Can I tell you, Stewart, that I rode my Harley to work one day and looked down to see that I had accidentally put on my son's shoes. I put on my son's shoes—his feet were the same size as mine—and I thought to myself, when did he grow up, and where was I?

"You know, Stewart, that doesn't come back: that time, the moments I sacrificed, they are gone. Every man has to decide for himself whether these sacrifices to wealth, or fame, or art are worth it, and you will make the right decision, because it will be yours. But please keep in mind, it might not have to be an all-or-nothing thing: it might be that as a chef, you will see your son grow to be a man, and you will have been there to see much of it."

As a proudly present father, not a day goes by that I don't thank Kunz for this pointed advice. When I consider the path I have chosen, the power of his words, I am grateful.

CHICKEN WINGS

SERVES 6–8

The marinade can be made two days ahead of time; refrigerate until ready to use. Do yourself a big favor: wrap your baking sheets with aluminum foil, something we would never do in the restaurant. At home, I'd rather spend my time eating wings than cleaning a pan.

3 cloves garlic, minced
½ Granny Smith apple, peeled and cored
2 tablespoons chopped ginger
2 tablespoons chopped lemongrass
2 green onions
¼ bunch cilantro, rinsed well

2 tablespoons sugar

2 tablespoons sake

¼ cup soy sauce

⅛ teaspoon freshly ground black pepper

2 tablespoons sesame oil

2 tablespoons orange juice

1 tablespoon honey

2½ tablespoons Sriracha

1½ teaspoons toasted sesame seeds

2½ pounds chicken wings and drummies

Cilantro sprigs, for garnish

1. Place garlic, apple, and ginger in bowl of a food processor; cover and pulse until well chopped. Add lemongrass, green onions, and cilantro; continue to pulse until almost smooth.

2. Transfer mixture to a large bowl; stir in next 9 ingredients (sugar through sesame seeds). Refrigerate at least 2 hours to allow flavors to meld.

3. Add chicken wings and drummies to mixture and marinate, refrigerated, at least 6 hours, or overnight.

To Cook:

1. Preheat oven to 450°F. Line a baking sheet with aluminum foil. Spread chicken evenly on baking sheet; discard excess marinade.

2. Bake 10 to 12 minutes; turn chicken parts and bake an additional 25 to 30 minutes, until the exteriors become nicely caramelized. Garnish with sprigs of cilantro; serve.

Chicken Wings

SPICED FOOTBALL POTATO CHIPS

SERVES 1–8

If you have to eat chips from time to time — and I know I do — make them yourself. It's easy, and you can snack on them guilt free. These chips go great with beer, which some of us also need to enjoy on occasion.

2 russet potatoes
1 quart canola oil
Chip Mix (p. 156)

1. Rinse, peel, and thinly slice potatoes. Immediately place slices in medium bowl filled with cold water and let stand for at least 1 hour. Drain and dry well.

2. Fill medium saucepan about one-third of the way with oil; heat to 275°F. Keeping the chips to a single layer in the pan, fry batches in hot oil until light golden brown.

3. Using a slotted spoon, remove chips from oil, drain on paper towels, and immediately and liberally sprinkle with Chip Mix. Enjoy while warm. Chips can be stored, but why would you want to?

Assembling spring rolls

SEARED SALMON SPRING ROLLS

MAKES 5–6 ROLLS

FOR MARINATED SALMON:
2 tablespoons soy sauce
¼ cup sesame oil
2 tablespoons rice wine vinegar
1½ tablespoons honey
1½ teaspoons onion powder
¾ teaspoon cayenne pepper

1½ teaspoons celery salt
1 pound salmon, cut in 1-inch strips
1 tablespoon canola oil

1. Place first 7 ingredients (soy sauce through celery salt) in a medium bowl and whisk until well combined. Pour over salmon and marinate, covered, in refrigerator 2 hours.

2. Preheat sauté pan over high heat, add canola oil, and heat to smoking point. Add salmon to the pan; discard marinade. Cook about 2 minutes, turning salmon occasionally to sear on all sides.

3. Remove salmon and pan juices to plate and let cool to about room temperature. Flake salmon with a fork and set aside with pan juices.

Seared Salmon Spring Roll

ASSEMBLY:
6 (8-inch) spring roll wrappers
About 24 to 30 cilantro leaves
2 tablespoons toasted sesame seeds
1 cucumber, peeled, seeded, and sliced into thin 3-by-¼-inch ribbons
About ½ cup Dipping Sauce (p. 152)

Fill large bowl with warm water. Working in batches, soak 1 to 3 spring roll wrappers in water until softened, about 2 minutes. Remove rounds from water and arrange in single layer on work surface. Place 4 to 5 cilantro leaves, ⅛ teaspoon toasted sesame seeds, and 2 cucumber ribbons down middle of each round. Place about ⅓ cup flaked salmon filling with juices on each round. Fold one edge of each round over filling. Fold in ends. Roll up rice paper rounds tightly. Transfer to platter. Repeat with remaining rounds. Slice spring rolls in half diagonally. Spoon about 1 tablespoon Dipping Sauce over each half. Serve immediately.

Until I worked for Eric Ripert, I thought that to be a good chef one had only to be a great cook. I spent years on that very quest, shuffling from one cooking challenge to the next.

Then Ripert came along and changed the way I looked at my career and my life. In the two and a half years that I worked for him, I made sous in a relatively short period of time and traveled extensively. I learned that to be a good chef I would also need to learn how to be a decent person, the quality that above all else would determine how and why people would choose to work with me and eat the food I had created. At the time I didn't have a clue about the long-term effect he was having on me and how he had given me the tools I would need to be the kind of person I could believe in. Sure, he may have led this horse to water, but he also taught it how to drink.

Often he would invite me to sit in his office and ask me questions about my mentality and my outlook. Frustrations, failures, successes. He rarely gave much advice, instead offering slight nudges in one direction or another. It was corporate therapy, through and through. But in those moments I learned more about how to manage myself and others than I have from anyone in my life.

A great chef like Eric Ripert brings out nascent qualities in others and can open up the world in ways that have nothing to do with being a great cook and everything to do with aspiring to discover inner beauty. This, the true gift of his career, has had a pronounced impact on our community.

I don't place myself in the category of great chef, not by a long shot, but I think about those discussions often, about the choices we make and how a person ought not be trapped in his or her own mythology. Life, according to Ripert, is the greatest work of art, and everybody can be a great artist. So when the fire struck and I sat and reflected upon my mentors and how they would react, I could see Ripert smiling at me and asking if there were perhaps other opportunities that excited me.

Foie and Lentil Crepes with Hibiscus Syrup

FOIE AND LENTIL CREPES WITH HIBISCUS SYRUP

SERVES 4

Specialty ingredient alert: the hibiscus is easy to find at most any mercado; the foie poses more of a challenge. Order it online, or ask the chef at your favorite restaurant for advice on local purveyors.

CREPES

½ cup whole milk
1 egg
½ cup all-purpose flour
⅛ teaspoon salt
1 tablespoon butter, melted and lightly browned

1. Combine all ingredients, in order listed, in container of electric blender; cover and blend until smooth, about 2 to 3 minutes. Pour mixture through fine-mesh strainer, discarding lumps. Allow to rest, refrigerated, at least 2 hours, preferably overnight.

2. Pour just enough batter to coat the bottom of a preheated small nonstick sauté pan set over medium heat, working quickly to swirl the pan and spread batter in one even layer. Tip out any excess batter, and use a spoon to crop the edges of the crepe to make it round.

3. When the crepe has set and is lightly brown on the bottom, about 2 minutes, flip with a spatula and lightly brown the other side. Remove crepe to a plate; repeat process with remaining batter. Cover crepes with plastic wrap and set aside.

FOR LENTILS:

1 tablespoon canola oil
1 small onion, minced
¼ cup sugar
1 tablespoon Curry Powder (p. 155)
½ cup black beluga lentils
2½ cups water
½ teaspoon salt

1. Heat oil in a large (3-quart) saucepan over medium heat; add onions and sweat 10 minutes, until brown. Add sugar and stir briefly; allow sugar to melt and brown, about 8 minutes.

2. Mix in Curry Powder and lentils. Add water and bring to a boil; reduce heat to maintain a simmer; cook 40 minutes. Remove from heat. Stir in salt; set aside.

HIBISCUS SYRUP

⅔ cup rice wine vinegar
⅔ cup sugar
3 tablespoons water
½ cup dried hibiscus

1. Combine vinegar and sugar in a medium saucepan over medium heat and reduce by half, about 15 minutes. The result will be slightly amber in color.

2. Add water and hibiscus; reduce heat to low and cook 4 minutes. Remove from heat, steep 5 minutes, and then strain, discarding solids, and allow syrup to cool. If necessary, syrup can be thinned with a little warm water.

FOR FOIE GRAS:

½ pound raw foie gras

1 teaspoon salt

1 teaspoon ground pepper

1. Carefully remove any visible veins from foie gras, taking care to avoid unduly scarring the exterior. Slice foie gras into 4 even portions using a knife dipped in hot water to prevent sticking. Freeze slices 5 to 10 minutes. Season with salt and pepper

2. Preheat a heavy, nonstick pan over high heat approximately 5 minutes. In batches of 1 to 2 slices, sear foie gras to rare, about 45 to 55 seconds per side. Do not crowd the pan. Remove to plate and set aside.

PRESENTATION:

Place crepe on a plate, top with a spoonful of lentils and slice of foie gras. Wrap crepe around filling and tie with a long chive, if desired. Finish with a drizzle of Hibiscus Syrup. Serve.

CHOPPED LIVER

SERVES 8

Don't make this recipe. No, I mean it. You will never look at liver the same way again; you may even consider yourself a fan. Don't say I didn't warn you.

1 pound chicken livers

1 cup whole milk

2 tablespoons canola oil, divided

½ cup minced shallot (about 3 shallots)

1 cup brandy

2 tablespoons butter

¼ teaspoon salt

Freshly ground black pepper

1. Rinse chicken livers and soak, refrigerated, in milk at least 8 hours or overnight.

2. Remove livers from milk and pat dry. Discard milk. Preheat a sauté pan large enough to hold livers without crowding them.

3. Heat 1 tablespoon canola oil and cook livers until lightly caramelized, about 4 to 5 minutes per side. Remove livers from pan to cool. Finely chop reserved livers, removing and discarding any connective tissue or sinew; set aside.

4. Reheat sauté pan over medium heat; add remaining canola oil and shallots. Sweat 3 to 4 minutes, until sexy and dark brown.

5. Remove pan from heat and add brandy; return pan to medium heat, standing clear and watching carefully to avoid igniting brandy. (If brandy ignites, don't panic: it will burn off quickly.) Reduce over high heat until nearly dry, about 3 minutes.

6. Add butter to pan while stirring shallots with a spatula. Season with salt and pepper to taste. Remove from heat and allow to cool. Combine mixture with chopped liver, and refrigerate until ready to use.

Serve chopped liver on toasted brioche or, for your leaner friends, on thin baguette slices.

When I started re-creating recipes for home use, I'll admit it hadn't occurred to me to read a recipe through in years. If I wanted to try something new, I'd review the list of ingredients and call the relevant purveyors and have the necessary items shipped to me. I never stopped to consider how long the dish would take to prepare or if I should start any steps in advance: I pretty much winged it, every time.

Then I started cooking at home, from old notebooks and even random scraps of paper shoved into the top drawer of my nightstand. On my fourth trip in a single day to the supermarket with my four-year-old, I started to get smart (*started* being the operative word). It occurred to me that if I spent less time being a cowboy about it, I could spend more time at the stove.

The recipes in this book represent years of work; they are tried and true. However, the one piece of advice I would give at the outset is this: noodle on the recipe before you get started. Doing so will just plain save you time and money and will make all the difference between enjoying your time in the kitchen and finding it burdensome.

BONE MARROW WITH CARROT JAM AND STEWED SWISS CHARD

SERVES 4

FOR BONE MARROW:

4 center-cut beef marrow bones, about 1½ to 2 pounds total
Good aged balsamic vinegar
Fleur de sel

Preheat oven to 400°F. Prepare bones by scraping away connective tissue. Place in roasting pan and bake 20 to 25 minutes. Sprinkle marrow with balsamic vinegar and fleur de sel. Set aside.

CARROT JAM WITH SWISS CHARD

1 tablespoon canola oil
4 carrots, chopped in ¼-inch pieces to yield about 1½ cups
1 medium onion, chopped in ¼-inch pieces to yield about 1 cup
2 tablespoons sugar
1 bunch Swiss chard, stems and ribs removed, sliced crosswise into 3-inch pieces, rinsed
    thoroughly, and soaked in cold water to remove grit
½ teaspoon salt
¼ teaspoon freshly ground black pepper

1. Heat oil in a medium sauté pan over high heat. Add carrots and onions, and cook and stir 5 minutes. Turn heat to low and continue to cook, stirring, an additional 8 minutes.

2. Add sugar and continue to cook an additional 10 minutes. Add raw, drained Swiss chard to pan with salt and pepper, increase heat to high, and cook until chard is wilted and tender, 5 to 6 minutes. Remove from heat.

FOR BAGUETTE BÂTONNETS:

½ par-cooked baguette

Preheat oven to 400°F. Halve baguette lengthwise, then cut into 4-by-¾-inch batons, about 12 to 16 total. Place on a small baking sheet and toast 10 to 12 minutes.

PRESENTATION:

Divide carrot jam among 4 plates, place a marrow bone on top of the jam, and serve with Baguette Bâtonnets. Poke bread sticks into the marrow, and soak up the greasy love.

*Bone Marrow with Carrot Jam
and Stewed Swiss Chard*

SALADS

SPINACH AND PISTACHIO SALAD WITH CRISPY SHALLOTS

SERVES 4

PISTACHIO PUREE

2 tablespoons canola oil

¼ cup unsalted pistachios, shelled

Puree ingredients in a blender 30 seconds. Set aside.

CRISPY SHALLOTS

2 medium shallots
½ tablespoon flour
2 cups canola oil
⅛ teaspoon salt

1. Trim top and root from shallots. Using a mandolin, slice shallots into thin rings about ⅛ inch thick. Toss shallot slices in flour until evenly coated.

2. Shake off excess flour and place shallots in small saucepan; cover with canola oil. Stir gently to break up rings.

3. Cook 10 minutes over medium heat, stirring occasionally, until shallots are light golden brown.

4. Remove shallots from pan with a slotted spoon and drain on paper towel; season with salt. Strain and reserve oil for use in vinaigrettes and dressings.

FOR SALAD:

⅛ teaspoon salt
½ teaspoon lemon juice
3 cups baby spinach, stems removed

Combine 2 teaspoons Pistachio Puree, salt, and lemon juice in a medium bowl. Whisk well. Add spinach and toss to coat. Stack spinach on 4 plates, top with crispy shallots, and drizzle with 1 tablespoon Pistachio Puree. Serve.

*Spinach and Pistachio Salad
with Crispy Shallots*

ARUGULA, ROASTED CAULIFLOWER, AND CHICKEN SALAD

SERVES 4

CHICKEN PARSLEY PATTIES

¾ pound boneless, skinless chicken thighs or ground chicken or turkey
1 teaspoon salt
¼ teaspoon freshly ground black pepper
1 tablespoon lemon juice
2 tablespoons finely chopped parsley
¾ teaspoon extra-hot Chinese mustard
¼ cup ice water
2 tablespoons canola oil

Arugula, Roasted Cauliflower, and Chicken Salad

1. If using whole thighs, process chicken through a quarter-inch grind plate. Repeat.

2. Place ground chicken in a medium bowl and add salt, pepper, lemon juice, parsley, and mustard. Mix well. Add ice water and mix for 1 minute. Shape mixture into 4 patties.

3. Heat oil in large sauté pan on medium-high heat. Cook patties until golden brown on both sides and centers are no longer pink, about 4 minutes per side. Set aside.

FOR ROASTED CAULIFLOWER:

3 tablespoons canola oil
½ head cauliflower, cut in ¾-inch pieces
¼ teaspoon salt

Place roasting pan in oven and preheat to 450°F. Place canola oil, cauliflower pieces, and salt in hot roasting pan. Cook about 30 minutes, stirring every 5 minutes, until golden brown. Remove cauliflower from pan and cool to room temperature, about 10 minutes.

PRESENTATION:

4 cups loosely packed baby arugula, rinsed well, stems removed

½ teaspoon salt

20 chives, cut into 1½-inch pieces

2 tablespoons extra-virgin olive oil

2 tablespoons lemon juice

½ cup Pecorino Romano slivers (thinly slice cheese with a vegetable peeler, then cut into julienne strips)

Freshly ground black pepper

1. Place arugula in a large bowl. Add cauliflower and salt to bowl; gently toss.

2. Add chives to salad along with olive oil and lemon juice; gently mix until well combined. Stir in Pecorino Romano.

3. Halve or quarter chicken patties and mix with arugula. Divide salad among 4 plates. Garnish with freshly ground black pepper. Serve.

BUTTERHEAD LETTUCE SALAD WITH FINGERLINGS AND FONTINA

SERVES 4

FOR FINGERLINGS:

1 pound fingerling potatoes

1 teaspoon salt

½ teaspoon whole black peppercorns

1 sprig thyme

Place potatoes, salt, peppercorns, and thyme in large saucepan, adding water to cover. Bring to simmer over medium heat, and cook 30 minutes, until tender (a knife will easily pierce the potatoes). Drain and cool potatoes. Peel potatoes with a paring knife, cut in half lengthwise, and set aside.

Butterhead Lettuce Salad with Fingerlings and Fontina

MUSTARD DRESSING

1 tablespoon Mayonnaise (p. 169)
1 tablespoon yogurt
¼ teaspoon lemon juice
2 teaspoons minced chives
⅛ teaspoon salt
1 tablespoon Mustard Vinaigrette (p. 150)

Whisk together all ingredients in a small bowl. Set aside.

FOR SALAD:

6 ounces fontina cheese, thinly shaved
3 to 4 leaves butterhead lettuce
1 teaspoon fleur de sel
½ teaspoon freshly ground black pepper
1 teaspoon minced chives

1. Preheat broiler. Combine potatoes and 2 tablespoons mustard dressing in medium bowl and mix well. Divide among 4 oven-safe plates.

2. Top potatoes with shaved fontina. Briefly place plates under broiler to slightly melt cheese.

3. Combine lettuce and remaining dressing in a medium bowl and mix. Divide lettuce among plates. Finish with fleur de sel, pepper, and chives. Serve.

BEET SALAD WITH SOY DRESSING

SERVES 4–6

Inspired by Jean-Georges but with my own twist, this dish brings back fond memories. It's the favorite warm dressing around our house, one that goes great with beets—and steak. The base makes enough for a couple more batches; save remainder for future use.

FOR BEETS:
10 (2- to 3-inch-diameter) beets, scrubbed clean and patted dry
¾ cup kosher salt

1. Preheat oven to 400°F. Shave off pointed end of each beet. Spread salt evenly on baking sheet; place beets atop salt. Roast beets 1¾ hours, or until easily pierced with a knife.

2. Remove beets from oven and, using a paper towel to hold hot beets, peel with a paring knife. Cool and set aside.

There is no better aptitude to creating great food than the ability to relax, to let ingredients blossom in their own time.

This quality does not come easily to me. My life is pedal to the metal, a hundred miles an hour, no time for breaks, sleep when I'm dead. So through the years I have had to teach myself to slow down, to watch the clock a little more, to remember that timing has to do as much with working quickly as it does with working slowly.

This admonition is never truer than when it comes to cooking beets. Such a beautiful vegetable, with its astounding complexity of flavor and characteristics, but oh, how it can be mishandled! An undercooked beet is a culinary crime of the highest order. It pays extraordinary dividends to listen to the beet that is about to be cooked, to its relative freshness or softness.

Of any vegetable people have said they disdain, beets have allowed me to win the most converts, mostly by cooking them with care and love, by giving them leave to slowly yield their mysteries. Be patient and remember to taste before you decide that they are done. Your family and friends will thank you.

Soy Dressing

½ cup light soy sauce
3 tablespoons rice wine
   vinegar
1 small shallot, peeled
   and thinly sliced
1 clove garlic, peeled
   and thinly sliced
¾ teaspoon whole
   black peppercorns
1½ teaspoons sugar
2¼ teaspoons freshly
   squeezed lemon
   juice

Beet Salad with Soy Dressing

1. Mix together all ingredients in medium saucepan; bring to a boil and then reduce heat to medium. Reduce liquid by one-quarter and then remove from heat.

2. Place mixture in an airtight container and allow to steep in refrigerator at least 8 hours or overnight.

3. Pour mixture through a fine-mesh strainer, discard solids, and set aside 3 tablespoons dressing, storing the remainder, refrigerated, for up to a month.

To finish the sauce:

4 tablespoons cold butter
1 tablespoon water
¼ teaspoon lemon juice

Place 3 tablespoons soy dressing in a medium saucepan and bring to simmer over medium heat. Gradually but rapidly whisk in cold butter. Whisk in lemon juice and water. Remove from heat. (Alternatively, for a smoother consistency, place hot liquid in a blender, add cold butter, cover, and process on high 10 seconds.)

Presentation:

Cut the beets into quarters or smaller, and arrange in the center of a plate. Drizzle sauce along the beets. For a twist, add chiffonade of napa cabbage: simply shave raw cabbage over the top of the dish. Serve.

GRILLED CAESAR SALAD

SERVES 4

This dressing variation I learned from Monsieur Ducasse. Leave it to the French guy to come up with the best Caesar.

CAESAR DRESSING

1½ tablespoons lemon juice

2 teaspoons Dijon-style mustard

1 anchovy

3 drops hot pepper sauce

1 clove garlic

1 soft-cooked egg (p. 33)

1½ teaspoons tomato paste

3 tablespoons water

⅔ cup grated Parmesan cheese

⅓ teaspoon kosher salt

⅓ teaspoon black pepper

⅓ cup canola oil

1. Combine lemon juice, Dijon-style mustard, anchovy, hot pepper sauce, and garlic in container of electric blender; cover and process 30 seconds.

2. Add egg, tomato paste, and water; blend 15 seconds. Add cheese and blend an additional 15 seconds. Add salt, pepper, and oil; blend 10 seconds. Set aside.

FOR GRILLED ROMAINE:

4 romaine hearts

1 tablespoon canola oil

¼ teaspoon kosher salt

¼ teaspoon black pepper

Preheat grill. Cut each romaine in half; brush cut side with canola oil and toss with salt and pepper. Place romaine cut side down on hot grill; cook 2 to 4 minutes, until romaine is charred but not burnt.

(recipe continues)

Grilled Caesar Salad

Fresh Parmesan
Cracked black pepper

Crisscross grilled romaine on each of 4 plates and, using the back of a spoon, spread 2 tablespoons Caesar Dressing over leaves or simply drizzle onto each plate. Shave on fresh Parmesan and crack a little more black pepper over each plate.

SHAVED FENNEL AND TUNA SALAD

SERVES 4

For this book, I have avoided including too many recipes that call for specialty ingredients. This one is the exception, but taking the extra trouble to order the truffle salt, Arroyabe del Norte tuna, and mustard oil (make sure it's the edible kind) online is well worth the effort. Another tip: the fresher the mushrooms, the easier they will be to slice.

Shaved Fennel and
Tuna Salad

FOR SALAD:

2 fennel bulbs, stems trimmed

10 button mushrooms, cleaned of dirt with a damp paper towel

10 medium spears asparagus

1 teaspoon canola oil

1. Preheat grill. Slice fennel and mushrooms with a mandolin into very thin pieces, about ⅛ inch thick. Set aside.

2. Cut asparagus into 2-inch pieces and toss with oil. Grill 3 minutes, rotating asparagus to prevent overcooking. Remove asparagus to plate and cool 5 minutes.

TO FINISH:

¼ cup currants

4 ounces olive oil–poached tuna, drained and flaked

¼ teaspoon fleur de sel

In large bowl, toss fennel, mushrooms, and asparagus with Vinaigrette. Gently fold currants and flaked tuna into salad. Divide salad among 4 plates, sprinkle with fleur de sel, and serve.

CHOPPED EGG AND TOAST WITH PEA GREENS

SERVES 4

I've never been a fan of adding butter to mashed eggs: a dash of salt or truffle salt will do, thank you. Incidentally, I found a phone app for cooking eggs that includes altitude and egg temperature in its calculation, but the app didn't work as well as this recipe will. Picture me blowing a raspberry in someone's general direction.

FOR EGGS:

4 eggs

1 teaspoon salt

1. Place eggs in medium saucepan with cold water to cover. Turn heat to high, bring to a boil, and allow to bubble for 1 minute. Remove from heat and leave eggs in the water 10 minutes.

2. Pour off hot water, cover eggs in cold water, and let sit 5 minutes. Peel eggs, place in medium bowl, add salt, and mash with a fork. Keep warm.

VINAIGRETTE

3 tablespoons mustard oil

1 tablespoon canola oil

2 tablespoons lemon juice

1 teaspoon honey

⅛ teaspoon truffle salt

Whisk all ingredients together in a small bowl. Set aside.

FOR TOAST:

1 loaf unsliced Pullman (square, white bread), cut into 4 (3-by-1-by-1-inch) croutons

2 tablespoons butter

2 tablespoons canola oil

⅛ teaspoon salt

⅛ teaspoon freshly ground black pepper

Heat butter and oil in sauté pan until frothy. Add all 4 croutons to pan and season with salt and pepper. Turn croutons to brown on all sides, about 1 minute per side. Remove from pan and drain on paper towel. Set aside.

PICKLED SHALLOT VINAIGRETTE

¼ cup Pickled Shallots (p. 157)

4 tablespoons water

⅓ cup canola oil

⅛ teaspoon cayenne pepper

½ teaspoon Dijon-style mustard

Combine all ingredients in container of an electric blender; cover and blend on high 30 seconds. Set aside 3 teaspoons of vinaigrette; refrigerate remaining in an airtight container for later use.

TO FINISH:

4 cups pea greens, rinsed, stems removed

1 teaspoon lemon juice

¾ teaspoon salt

Freshly ground black pepper

1. Combine pea greens, 3 teaspoons vinaigrette, lemon juice, and salt in a large bowl; toss well. Divide among 4 plates.

2. Spread each toasted crouton with mashed egg and place atop dressed pea shoots. Garnish with freshly ground black pepper. Serve.

Chopped Egg and Toast with Pea Greens

When I was eighteen, I took the train from my home in Montreal to Vancouver — more specifically Chilliwack — to visit one of my brothers for the summer. A military man, he had moved around. When he finally settled, I made a break for it to see him and his family. He set me up with a few job leads, but when nothing panned out in the first few days, someone suggested I pick strawberries for some spending cash.

How hard could it be? After all, we often joined my mother to help out at the local strawberry farm when it was jam season. We collected plenty of strawberries, our participation made my mother very happy, and we also ate a ton of fruit.

I can't legitimately claim that I have not had a privileged life. There were times I felt over-worked, hungry, and poor, but, truthfully, had I pulled the rip cord I would have received help immediately. No experience in my entire life brought that fact home like those two days on my hands and knees for hours in the mud from the morning dew or in the hot sun of midday, seeking too few strawberries ready for harvest. I worked rows next to "migrant workers" (what a laughable phrase that is, implying that they enjoy traveling around and working, like some folks enjoy visiting the Grand Canyon). I made about thirteen dollars that I never collected. Two days into it I received an offer to work in a provincial park in British Columbia, and I spent the summer cleaning campers' outhouses — grateful to have landed even this grubby assignment. Those jobs were the only two outside the biz I ever held.

To this day I feel guilty when I eat strawberries, but their provenance and that of so many items in our supermarkets is the same. A person picked it, and it's not nice work — in fact, it's downright shitty — and it has to get done. We should love and respect the items picked and the people who pick them. We honor them both when we make that food as beautiful and nourishing as possible.

SALMON SALAD

SERVES 6–8

This wonderful little dish is perfect for enjoying on the porch in the summer. And it's tailor-made for folks who don't love the taste of fish: poaching salmon in white wine removes all fishy flavor.

2 cups white wine
1 medium shallot, peeled and thinly sliced
1 pound salmon (trim okay)
1½ ounces smoked salmon, chopped
1 tablespoon minced chives
½ cup Mayonnaise (p. 169)
1 tablespoon Dijon-style mustard
1 tablespoon lemon juice
¼ teaspoon salt
White bread, thinly sliced and lightly toasted
Butter lettuce
Orange Powder (p. 155) to finish, if desired

1. Place wine and shallots in a small (1-quart) saucepan over high heat and bring to a boil. Reduce heat to low. Add fresh salmon to wine and cook until medium rare, about 10 to 15 minutes. Remove salmon and shallots from poaching liquid; refrigerate until cool. Discard liquid.

2. When salmon is cool, combine with next 6 ingredients (smoked salmon through salt), mix well, and refrigerate up to 2 days.

3. Serve salad open faced on toasted bread slices with a leaf or two of butter lettuce. Sprinkle with a pinch of Orange Powder, if desired.

Salmon Salad

MARINATED KOHLRABI SALAD

SERVES 4

1 pound kohlrabi
¼ small red onion
½ tablespoon fresh lemon juice
2 teaspoons fresh lime juice
¼ teaspoon salt
2 tablespoons extra-virgin olive oil
2½ tablespoons capers, drained and chopped
2 cups loosely packed Bibb lettuce

1. Peel kohlrabi and slice very thin; place in a large bowl. Slice onion very thin, rinse through a strainer, and pat dry. Stir into kohlrabi.

2. Stir in lemon and lime juices and salt; set mixture aside and allow to macerate 10 minutes.

3. Stir in oil and capers, toss with lettuce, and serve immediately.

SOUPS

TROPICAL MUSHROOM SOUP

SERVES 4–6

This recipe calls for many ingredients, yes, but the technique is easy, and you will love the results. This soup would make a tasty middle course in a summer meal featuring shellfish.

½ red bell pepper
½ green bell pepper
½ yellow bell pepper
1 tablespoon butter
¼ medium onion, sliced ¼ inch thick

*Tropical
Mushroom Soup*

½ stalk lemongrass, bruised and thinly sliced

2 cloves garlic, thinly sliced

1 inch fresh ginger root, finely grated

1 pound button mushrooms, rinsed quickly in cold water, patted dry, and thinly sliced

½ teaspoon salt

2 cups water, divided

½ bunch cilantro, rinsed well in cold water and patted dry; reserve about 20 leaves for garnish

1 (6-ounce) can pineapple juice, divided

1 (14-ounce) can coconut milk

¼ teaspoon red pepper flakes

¼ cup soy sauce

1½ teaspoons canola oil

1. Slice off tops and bottoms of each pepper and set aside for soup. Slice remaining peppers into ¼-inch slices to be used for garnish.

2. Melt butter in a stockpot over medium heat; add onion, lemongrass, garlic, ginger, and pepper trim. Cook 10 minutes, stirring occasionally.

3. Add mushrooms and salt to pot. Cook 25 minutes, until all liquid has evaporated. Add 1¾ cups water, cilantro, half the pineapple juice, coconut milk, red pepper flakes, and soy sauce; bring to a boil. Simmer 10 minutes; remove from heat.

4. Working in batches, fill container of electric blender to ⅓ capacity, cover and blend soup for 1 minute on high, and then strain. Return blended soup to stove to keep warm, or freeze in an airtight container up to 3 months.

5. For garnish, cook and stir pepper slices in canola oil in sauté pan over high heat about 7 minutes. Add remaining water and pineapple juice; cover. Allow to stew over medium heat about 6 minutes, until liquid has reduced and peppers have acquired a marmalade consistency. Remove from heat.

6. Place sautéed pepper slices in the center of each soup bowl. Ladle soup over peppers. Garnish with cilantro leaves. Serve.

PEA SOUP

Makes about 1 quart; serves 4

Years ago, during a construction delay at the opening of Ducasse at the Essex House, I spent a few weeks at Cafe Boulud to keep up my chops. One evening, a young cook messed up the pea soup by adding too much bay leaf. The soup was discarded, of course, but before he tossed it I sneaked over for a taste. The idea for this recipe was born in that instant. Peas and bay leaf, oh my: you'll want to bathe in this stuff. Keep it simple: you might even convince the pea haters in the crowd to give this one a try.

1¼ cups half-and-half
2 cups water
1 fresh bay leaf, rib removed
1 pound frozen peas, thawed
1 teaspoon salt

Combine half-and-half and water in a large saucepan; bring to a boil. Add bay leaf. Add peas and return to boiling. Remove from heat, place soup in container of electric blender, and add salt. Cover and blend until smooth, about 3 minutes. Serve.

SHRIMP SOUP

Serves 4

Shrimp Wontons
1 (12-ounce) package wonton wrappers
12 large (26/30) shrimp (about ½ pound), peeled and deveined
1 tablespoon cold butter, cut into 12 pieces
Cayenne pepper
Salt

1. Moisten edges of 1 wonton wrapper with a little water. Place 1 shrimp in the middle of the wrapper, top with 1 piece butter, and season with pinch of cayenne and salt.

(recipe continues)

Shrimp Soup

2. Fold two opposite corners of wrapper together to form triangle. Pinch edges together to seal. Set aside on a plate or baking sheet.

3. Repeat with remaining wonton wrappers and shrimp. Set aside.

FOR SOUP:
1 onion, thinly sliced
1 teaspoon black peppercorns
1 star anise
1 shallot, thinly sliced
1 stalk lemongrass, thinly sliced
5 cloves garlic, thinly sliced
1 teaspoon brown sugar
2 cups Shrimp Stock (p. 160)
1 cup water
½ teaspoon salt
1 teaspoon fish sauce

1. Heat a medium (2-quart) saucepan over high heat about 4 minutes, until very hot. Add onion and cook, stirring frequently, until dark brown.

2. Add black peppercorns, star anise, and shallot; cook 2 minutes. Add lemongrass, garlic, and brown sugar; reduce heat to medium and cook an additional 2 minutes.

3. Add Shrimp Stock, water, and salt; bring to a boil and simmer 15 minutes.

4. Remove from heat, add fish sauce, and let soup steep 10 minutes. Strain, discarding solids, and set aside.

TO FINISH:
1 (3½-ounce) package enoki mushrooms, 2-inch tops reserved, remainder discarded
¼ cup cilantro leaves
1 tablespoon minced chives

1. Heat soup to simmering in a medium saucepan over medium heat. Add wontons and simmer 3 to 4 minutes.

2. Remove wontons with a slotted spoon and divide among 4 bowls. Cover wontons with equal portions of soup. Top with enoki mushrooms, cilantro leaves, and chives. Serve.

Alain Ducasse is a giant among chefs. I met him one afternoon at Le Bernardin. The conference was top secret: I wasn't to reveal any details about his plans to open a New York restaurant. Eric Ripert and I took the elevator to the private room on the second floor, where we found Monsieur Ducasse dining.

He shook my hand, took a step back and gave me the once-over, then leaned in close, looked me in the eye, and whispered, "Eric says you have agreed to be my sous-chef in New York." "Oui, Chef." "Eric says you will work hard." "Oui, Chef." "Do you promise to work hard?" "Oui, Chef." With thanks we shook hands again, and it was decided.

Months later, a plane ticket arrived in the mail, letting me know when I would fly out of New York and that I would start my work for him in Monaco. I touched down in Nice and began in the kitchen a few hours later. In the moments, days, and weeks that followed, the most important lesson I learned was this: you *can* live the life you've imagined.

I would later fly to Paris to work in the kitchen at 16 Raymond Poincaré before returning to New York to help with the opening of Alain Ducasse at the Essex House. Working in his two kitchens in Europe was a turning point in my career and life. It was as if I had scaled the mountain and, having reached the tip-top, realized that the kitchen I had imagined as nearly perfect did in fact exist. His kitchens ran at a very high level, people busied about with great proficiency in their craft, and there was none of the all-too-common sense of entitlement that so many cooks stateside seem to feel. It was deeply moving and as near to perfect as I had experienced and have since, inspiring in me a conviction to set out to do it "my way."

LETTUCE SOUP

SERVES 4

I know this recipe sounds ridiculous, but it is quite yummy, and, frankly, if you've had salad a few nights in a row, this combination can provide a nice break.

3 leaves romaine lettuce
2 leaves iceberg lettuce
1½ cups half-and-half
1 bay leaf
⅛ teaspoon freshly ground black pepper
¾ teaspoon salt
⅛ teaspoon cayenne pepper
1 tablespoon Crème Fraîche (p. 166)
⅛ teaspoon star anise powder

Lettuce Soup

1. Bring 3 quarts water and 2 tablespoons salt to a boil in a large saucepan. Blanch romaine and iceberg lettuce 5 seconds in boiling salted water; drain and rinse under cold water until cool. Set aside.

2. Bring remaining ingredients (half-and-half through star anise powder) to a boil in a medium saucepan. Remove from heat and place mixture in container of electric blender along with blanched lettuces. Cover and process until smooth. Serve.

SUMMER SAKE SOUP

SERVES 4

This soup, with its strong and lingering flavor, is a fine dish for a hot summer night. I prepare just enough for four people — and make them beg for more.

2 cups watermelon juice (store-bought or, better yet, prepared by pureeing watermelon in a food
   processor and pressing the result through a fine-mesh strainer)
½ cup sake
½ teaspoon freshly grated ginger
½ teaspoon honey
½ teaspoon fish sauce
½ teaspoon salt, plus more to taste

Whisk together all ingredients in a medium bowl; season with additional salt if necessary.

PRESENTATION:
1 cup Pickled Shiitake Mushrooms (p. 159), finely sliced
4 Grilled Shrimp (p. 157), finely chopped
Mint Oil (p. 159)

Divide Pickled Shiitake Mushrooms and Grilled Shrimp among 4 bowls and ladle in equal
portions of soup. Finish with a drizzle of Mint Oil and serve.

PARSNIP AND SAGE SOUP

MAKES ABOUT 1½ QUARTS; SERVES 6–8

1 tablespoon canola oil
1½ pounds parsnip, peeled and chopped
18 Arabica coffee beans
½ cup sake
⅓ cup heavy cream
5 cups water
2 teaspoons salt
8 sage leaves

1. Add canola oil to a medium saucepan and heat on low; add parsnips and cook until lightly
   caramelized, about 30 minutes.

2. Add coffee beans and sweat 5 minutes. Add sake and turn heat to high; reduce until almost all liquid has evaporated, about 2 minutes. Add cream, water, and salt; bring to a boil and simmer 10 minutes. Remove from heat and add sage.

3. Working in batches, place soup in container of electric blender; cover and process until smooth. Strain, discarding solids, and serve.

CREAM OF MUSSEL SOUP WITH TOMATOES

MAKES 1 QUART; SERVES 6–8

"This is a simple and elegant recipe, great for a dinner party," Heidi noted on this recipe, the only one she commented on. I caught her one night sneaking this soup out of a coffee mug all by herself in the dark. I followed the groans.

1 teaspoon canola oil
3 cloves garlic, chopped and mixed with ½ teaspoon salt to make a paste
¾ cup Tomato Fondue (p. 167)
1 recipe Mussel Stock (p. 164)
1 cup water
1 cup heavy cream
1 teaspoon salt
2 tablespoons chopped parsley

Heat a large saucepan over high heat; add oil and sweat garlic paste until fragrant. Add Tomato Fondue, Mussel Stock, water, and cream and bring to a boil. Remove from heat. Season with salt, stir in parsley, and serve.

SMOKED BLACK-EYED PEA SOUP

MAKES ABOUT 2 QUARTS; SERVES 8–12

Delicious and easy. Make the full batch and freeze half of it: you'll thank me in January.

1 tablespoon canola oil
1 medium onion, finely chopped
1 head garlic, peeled and minced
1½ pounds smoked pork hocks
1½ cups dried black-eyed peas
8 cups water
2 teaspoons salt
⅛ teaspoon red pepper flakes
1 tablespoon champagne vinegar
⅛ teaspoon black pepper
½ cup Tomato Fondue (p. 167)
1½ tablespoons fish sauce

1. Heat oil in a large (4-quart) saucepan and cook onion, stirring, 4 to 5 minutes. Add garlic and sweat until fragrant. Remove from heat and place mixture in slow cooker.

2. Add hocks, peas, and water to slow cooker; cover and cook on low 5 to 6 hours. Remove hocks: separate meat from the bone, skin, and fat; finely chop meat and set aside for the soup. Discard bones, skin, and fat.

3. Remove fat from soup's surface by skimming with a ladle; discard fat.

4. Stir together remaining ingredients (salt through fish sauce) and hock meat in a large saucepan over high heat. Cook 15 minutes, until hot, and serve immediately. Really, this soup is also terrific to have in the freezer. Store up to 3 months.

PIZZA & PASTA

PIZZA DOUGH

MAKES 8 PIZZAS

The kids love this one, and so do I. It's a great interactive dish as well. If you like the crusts a little sweeter, brush on some honey after grilling.

Grilled pizza crusts

1 package (2½ teaspoons) instant dry yeast
1 cup warm water
3 cups all-purpose flour
1½ teaspoons salt
1 teaspoon sugar
4 teaspoons extra-virgin olive oil, plus extra for grilling

1. Dissolve yeast in warm water 5 minutes.

2. Combine flour, salt, and sugar in bowl of standing mixer fitted with a dough hook. Add yeast mixture to dry ingredients and mix until elastic; alternatively, mix by hand on a cutting board.

3. Cover with plastic wrap and allow to rest in a warm spot in the kitchen — on top of the fridge works well — 1½ hours.

4. Cut dough into 8 equal portions, rub with olive oil, cover, and allow to rest an additional 30 minutes.

5. Flatten dough into 10-inch circles with a rolling pin. (Recipe can be prepared ahead to this point: place rounds between parchment paper and refrigerate.) Preheat grill. Lightly brush both sides of dough rounds with oil and grill 2 minutes per side. Follow instructions for preparations that follow.

At Ducasse in Paris, the purveyors would display their produce, fish, meat, what have you in the kitchen and await the arrival of the chef de cuisine, then Jean-François Piège. One particular morning, I spied through the garde manger window a wooden box that looked to contain about four pounds of beautiful black truffles.

That day I was directed to clean the truffles, and I was elated. Truffles emit a gorgeous scent — earthy, funky, sexy, sweet. I was stationed in a back corner of the kitchen; over a sink we had placed a fine-mesh tami to catch any chunks that might fall off. Armed with only a toothbrush and a steady trickle of water to help lubricate bits of earth that refused to yield their hold, I cleaned.

There I stood for about a month. The truffle guy. I organized, cleaned, cut, jarred, and peeled truffles for the season. At the end of that month, my arms were locked into a set position, my back screamed in pain from standing over the sink, and my fingers, arthritic from the running cold water, would barely open and close. Yet for all of that, I never for a single moment felt anything but great joy at being in the presence of these little jewels from the earth.

Too few are familiar with the truffle, and many have been turned off by random negative run-ins with cheap truffle oil. We can all work to remedy this great tragedy through the judicious use of all things truffle.

Truffle and Honey Pizza

TRUFFLE AND HONEY PIZZA

SERVES 4

1 (.875-ounce) tube summer truffle puree
2 cloves and 1 tablespoon oil from Garlic Confit (p. 166)
1 tablespoon warm water
⅛ teaspoon salt
1 tablespoon honey
1 8-ounce Pizza Dough portion (p. 52), grilled
1½ ounces Grana Padano

1. Make truffle "sauce" by combining truffle puree, Garlic Confit and oil, water, salt, and honey and mixing with a fork until smooth. Spread truffle sauce evenly over grilled Pizza Dough.

2. Using a vegetable peeler, shave Grana Padano across top of pizza. Cut into 8, take one for the cook, and spread the love.

GRILLED ZUCCHINI AND BASIL PIZZA

SERVES 4

2 small zucchini, scrubbed clean and sliced lengthwise into ¼-inch slices
½ cup Citrus Vinaigrette (p. 151), divided
1 8-ounce Pizza Dough portion (p. 52), grilled
12 small basil leaves
⅛ teaspoon fleur de sel
⅛ teaspoon red pepper flakes

1. Preheat grill to medium-high. Toss zucchini slices with 5 tablespoons Citrus Vinaigrette and marinate 15 to 20 minutes. Remove zucchini from marinade; discard marinade.

2. Grill zucchini until well marked and tender, about 3 minutes per side. Slice zucchini into ¼-inch strips. Set aside.

3. Spread remaining Citrus Vinaigrette on grilled Pizza Dough, add grilled zucchini, and finish with basil leaves, fleur de sel, and red pepper flakes. Serve.

SHRIMP AND CILANTRO PIZZA

SERVES 4

3 tablespoons Cilantro Pesto (p. 150)
1 8-ounce Pizza Dough portion (p. 52), grilled
8 Poached Shrimp (p. 156), sliced in half lengthwise
3 tablespoons finely grated Grana Padano
⅛ teaspoon red pepper flakes

Spread Cilantro Pesto evenly on grilled Pizza Dough. Top with Poached Shrimp, Grana Padano, and red pepper flakes. Cut into 8 slices, unless you and your guests are close friends.

Shrimp and Cilantro Pizza

PASTA DOUGH

MAKES 1½ POUNDS; SERVES 12

2 cups bread flour
½ cup all-purpose flour
1 teaspoon salt
4 egg yolks
3 tablespoons extra-virgin olive oil
½ cup cold water

1. Place both flours and salt in the bowl of a standing mixer fitted with a dough hook. In a separate bowl, whisk together yolks, oil, and water.

2. With mixer set to low, slowly add liquids, over the course of 6 to 7 minutes. Continue mixing on low about 15 additional minutes, or until ingredients are fully incorporated.

3. Shape dough into a ball and wrap tightly with plastic wrap. Let rest 45 minutes.

4. Cut the pasta into three equal chunks and wrap tightly in plastic. Store in the refrigerator for 1 to 2 days or in the freezer for up to 3 months. Follow instructions for preparations that follow.

PAPPARDELLE PASTA

SERVES 4

⅓ recipe Pasta Dough (p. 56)
Flour for dusting

1. Roll out ½ cup Pasta Dough on work surface lightly dusted with flour. Use flour sparingly.

2. Using a pasta machine, process dough 3 times on the widest setting, 2 times on the next smallest setting, and 3 times on the smallest setting, until pasta is ¹⁄₁₆ inch thick. Repeat with remaining dough.

3. Using a pizza wheel, cut pasta sheet into ½-inch strips and then cut strips into ¾-inch-long pieces. Follow instructions for preparing pasta on page 61.

Making pappardelle pasta

TROFIETTE PASTA

SERVES 4

⅓ recipe Pasta Dough (p. 56)
Flour for dusting

1. Start with ½ cup Pasta Dough. Using a pasta machine and just enough flour to prevent sticking, run dough through the widest setting 3 times, the next smallest 1 time, and the next smallest 3 times, until the pasta sheet is about ⅛ inch thick.

2. Using a pizza wheel, cut pasta sheet into 6-by-1-inch strips. Grasp individual pasta pieces at each end, twist, and crimp to hold shape — like a Twizzler.

3. Repeat with remaining dough. Follow instructions for preparing pasta on page 65.

Making trofiette pasta

"You are like a fucking donkey, a mule. For you that means something bad, but it's not. Your true gift lies in how much of a workhorse you are." With that, Eric Ripert turned and walked away. We had returned the night before from a trip to Peru, where we had worked for a solid week taking over a Lima kitchen. Arriving at the airport late on Sunday evening, I was back at work in the kitchen on Monday at 10 AM. Ripert took the morning off, and by dinnertime when he came in, he was exhausted. I wasn't.

Parents will sometimes tell me their kids want to go to culinary school, want to be chefs. I always offer the same advice, and I'll repeat it here. The fact is that few people listen, probably because the truth just ain't pretty.

They're gonna have to work very hard, harder than at a lot of other jobs. They will need to work evenings, holidays, any time folks are out celebrating, period. Compensation will be minimal. Probably they think they will be the exception, and maybe they will: perhaps they can get on a TV show that does an end run around the hard work. But it's not likely, and if there is a shortcut, they'll need to be sure they want to take it. The reality of doing this work professionally is bleak.

If they are anything like me — not the sharpest knife in the drawer, not the best looking or the most talented — they need to be able to do only one thing: work hard. Not just harder than the next guy, but as hard as they possibly can. Good things may happen — they may be among the few who own a successful restaurant, who are financially secure — but without doing the backbreaking work, the only thing guaranteed is even bleaker. As they decide whether to cook professionally, advise them to consider very carefully the following: nothing is owed them. If they complain that it's unfair when the joker next to them is promoted over them, do them a favor: remind them that much will be expected of them but they themselves should not expect much.

BRAISED OXTAIL WITH LEMON AND GOLDEN BEETS WITH PAPPARDELLE PASTA

SERVES 4

You can start the oxtails the night before and even prepare the beets in advance.

FOR OXTAILS:

2 pounds oxtails

1 teaspoon salt

2 tablespoons canola oil

½ onion, cut side caramelized with a hand torch or under the broiler until very dark

3 cloves garlic

3 whole cloves

10 black peppercorns

Braised Oxtail with Lemon and Golden Beets with Pappardelle Pasta

1. Season oxtails with salt. Heat oil in a large sauté pan over medium-high heat. Sear oxtails until brown on all sides, rotating constantly, about 10 minutes.

2. Place oxtails in slow cooker, add remaining ingredients (onion through peppercorns), and cover with cold water (about 3 cups). Cook on low 12 hours.

3. When oxtails are tender, remove from liquid and cool to room temperature. Pick meat off the bone and set aside. Discard bones, gristle, and fat.

4. Separate fat from cooking liquid and strain liquid into a medium saucepan, discarding solids. Over medium-low heat, reduce liquid to about ½ cup, about 20 minutes. Set aside.

FOR BEETS:

1 bunch (3 to 4) golden beets, greens attached

1. Bring a large saucepan of salted water to a boil. Remove greens from beets. Rinse and soak greens in cold water until no grit remains.

2. Rinse and peel beets. Quarter beets lengthwise, then thinly slice crosswise.

3. Blanch beet greens in boiling water until tender, about 4 to 5 minutes. Remove greens from pot and run under cold water. Squeeze greens dry and cut into ½-inch slices. Set aside.

4. Blanch sliced beets in the same boiling water 8 to 10 minutes, until tender yet firm. Remove from pot and quickly rinse under cold water.

TO FINISH:

1 recipe Pappardelle Pasta (p. 56)
½ recipe Beurre Fondue (p. 169)
½ cup finely grated Grana Padano cheese, plus more for garnish, if desired
1 teaspoon lemon juice

1. Bring pot of water to a boil; add pinch of salt. Add Pappardelle Pasta to water and cook 1 to 3 minutes, until tender but firm. Drain pasta.

2. Place cooked pasta into large sauté pan of Beurre Fondue with beet tops and bottoms and oxtail meat and sauce and toss. Add cheese and lemon juice; toss again.

3. Divide pasta among 4 bowls. Finish with additional cheese as desired. Serve.

VEGETARIAN "BOLOGNESE"

SERVES 4

This dish was an instant hit when we opened Heidi's. Don't be tempted to skimp on the butter: your friends will thank you.

"BOLOGNESE"

1 ounce dried mushrooms (porcinis, shiitake, morel)
½ tablespoon canola oil
1 cup finely chopped celery
1 cup finely chopped carrot
1 cup finely chopped onion
2 cloves garlic, thinly sliced
1 teaspoon salt
½ teaspoon red pepper flakes
1 (14½-ounce) can diced tomatoes
2 cups red wine

1. Rehydrate dried mushrooms in 2 cups hot water. Repeat as needed to cleanse mushrooms of sand. Be sure to lift mushrooms out of the water, rather than pouring liquid and mushrooms through a strainer.

2. Heat canola oil in large saucepan over low to medium heat. Add celery and cook 5 minutes, then add carrot and cook another 5 minutes, then add onion and cook an additional 8 minutes.

3. Add garlic, salt, and red pepper flakes; cook 2 minutes, until garlic is slightly colored. Chop rehydrated mushrooms; add to pan and sweat 1 minute. Add undrained tomatoes and simmer 10 minutes.

4. Add wine and bring to a boil; simmer 15 minutes. Remove from heat. Set aside ¾ cup sauce. Freeze remaining sauce in airtight container for up to 3 months.

FOR PASTA:

1 recipe Pappardelle Pasta (p. 56)
1 recipe Beurre Fondue (p. 169)
⅛ teaspoon salt
⅛ teaspoon freshly ground black pepper

Bring pot of water to a boil; add pinch of salt. Add Pappardelle Pasta; cook for 1 minute, until tender but firm. Drain pasta; toss with Beurre Fondue and salt and pepper. Set aside.

(recipe continues)

Vegetarian "Bolognese"

To finish:

4 tablespoons butter

1 cup water

Extra-virgin olive oil

¼ cup grated Grana Padano or Parmesan cheese

Freshly ground black pepper

1. Heat sauté pan over medium heat. Add ¾ cup "Bolognese," butter, and water; swirling pan, reduce to sauce-like consistency, about 4 to 5 minutes. Remove from heat.

2. Divide pasta among 4 bowls. Spoon sauce over noodles. Drizzle with extra-virgin olive oil, grated cheese, and pepper. Serve and enjoy. Don't tell your doctor.

TROFIETTE WITH ROAST POBLANO, FRESH MOZZARELLA, AND CELERY PESTO

SERVES 4

For roasted poblano:

1 poblano pepper, rinsed and patted dry

1. Roast pepper over open flame until blackened — skin blistered but pepper not burned.

2. Place pepper in plastic container with tight-fitting lid and let sit 25 minutes.

3. Working over a cutting board, peel and discard skin and slice pepper in 2½-by-½-inch strips. Set aside.

Celery Pesto

½ cup Italian (flat) parsley leaves

1 clove garlic

⅛ teaspoon salt

⅛ teaspoon cracked black pepper

¼ cup extra-virgin olive oil

2 tablespoons grated Grana Padano or Parmesan cheese

1½ tablespoons pine nuts, toasted

2 celery ribs plus 2 tablespoons celery leaves

1. Combine parsley, garlic, salt, and pepper in bowl of small food processor; cover and process until minced, about 1 minute.

2. Add olive oil and Grana Padano or Parmesan and process 1 minute. Add pine nuts and pulse to roughly chop. Remove mixture from processor bowl and set aside.

Trofiette with Roast Poblano, Fresh Mozzarella, and Celery Pesto

3. Peel celery ribs and slice on bias to ⅛ inch thick. Bring medium saucepan of salted water to a boil. Add celery and blanch 1 minute; drain. Rinse celery under cold water and pat dry. Fold blanched celery and celery leaves into pesto. Set aside.

FOR PASTA:

1 recipe Trofiette Pasta (p. 58)

Bring pot of water to a boil; add pinch of salt. Add Trofiette Pasta and cook 2 minutes, until tender but firm. Drain pasta, reserving about ½ cup cooking water for finishing the sauce.

⟫⟩●⟨⟪

PRESENTATION:

½ cup thinly sliced celery

¼ cup grated Grana Padano

4 ounces fresh mozzarella, cut into ½-inch batons

Celery leaves for garnish

1. Stir together roasted poblano pieces, sliced celery, celery pesto, and ½ cup reserved pasta water in a large saucepan over medium heat; warm through. Add Grana Padano and toss. Add pasta and toss to combine. Stir in mozzarella. Remove from heat.

2. Divide pasta and sauce among 4 bowls. Garnish with celery leaves. Serve.

RAVIOLI

MAKES 24 PIECES; SERVES 4

1 recipe Pasta Dough (p. 56)
Flour for dusting
1 recipe Butternut Squash Filling (p. 68)
Cornmeal for storing finished raviolis

Preparing Ravioli

1. Using about ½ cup Pasta Dough at a time, lightly dust with flour and press into a 4-by-2-inch rectangle.

2. Using a pasta machine and just enough flour to prevent sticking, run dough through the widest setting 3 times, the next smallest 1 time, and the next smallest 3 times, until the pasta sheet is about ⅛ inch thick. Repeat with remaining dough.

3. Trim dough sheet to about 5 by 18 inches. Along center of dough sheet, place about 1 tablespoon Butternut Squash Filling at 2½-inch intervals. Using a small amount of water, gently moisten a ring around each filling.

4. Fold the dough sheet over and seal tightly around each filling using the side of your hand. Using a 2-inch round cutter or a pastry wheel, cut out ravioli shape. Press edges to seal; discard pasta trim.

5. Repeat process with remaining dough and filling. Store ravioli on cornmeal-lined baking sheet until ready to cook.

6. Follow instructions for preparing pasta on page 69.

When I worked for Jean-Georges Vongerichten, there was not a day I wasn't excited about getting off the subway at One Central Park West, the home of JG's flagship restaurant.

There is a chef's public persona and then the private man behind it, and what a joy it was to work for both. Not only because he was a great cook, or because his language of food was profound, but because his personality was so much fun. It's hard to imagine him without a mischievous and wonderful smile on his face, bounding through the dining room at a breakneck pace.

His style of cooking paid attention less to technique and more to intention, to being in the right place emotionally in order to create beauty. Some of the technique was downright goofy, yet the results were astounding. In the realm of life lessons I picked up from these many chefs, I can think of none more profound, none more enduring, than to have fun, laugh, and enjoy. It will show in your food.

BUTTERNUT SQUASH RAVIOLI

MAKES ABOUT 24 RAVIOLIS; SERVES 4–5

BUTTERNUT SQUASH FILLING
1½ pounds butternut squash, peeled, seeded, and cut into 1½-inch chunks
½ teaspoon salt
¼ cup canola oil
⅛ teaspoon ground cinnamon
½ cup maple syrup
1 recipe Ravioli (p. 66)

1. Heat a large oven-safe skillet in oven at 350°F for 10 minutes. Toss squash chunks with salt.

2. Add oil to skillet and heat 5 minutes. Add squash and roast in oven 30 minutes, until golden brown, stirring occasionally. Add cinnamon and maple syrup to skillet; return to oven 5 minutes.

3. Remove squash from oven and cool slightly. Puree in a food processor 2 minutes, until smooth. Refrigerate squash puree in an airtight container until completely chilled, at least 3 hours.

4. Fill Ravioli as instructed on page 66.

To cook ravioli and finish:

2 tablespoons extra-virgin olive oil

2 tablespoons aged balsamic vinegar

¼ cup grated Grana Padano

¼ cup Italian (flat) parsley leaves

1. Bring pot of water to a boil; add pinch of salt. Working in batches, add ravioli to pot and boil until pasta floats, about 3 minutes. Remove with slotted spoon; repeat with remaining ravioli.

2. Divide ravioli among 4 plates. Drizzle ravioli with olive oil, balsamic vinegar, Grana Padano, and parsley leaves. Serve immediately.

GNOCCHI

Makes about 3 cups

1 pound russet potatoes, peeled

1 teaspoon salt, divided

⅛ teaspoon black pepper

1 egg

½ cup all-purpose flour, plus 1 cup for rolling and cutting dough

1 tablespoon canola oil

1. Place potatoes in large saucepan and cover with cold water; add ¼ teaspoon salt. Bring to a boil; reduce heat and simmer until tender. (While potatoes are cooking, prepare the rest of the ingredients: you'll want to work quickly through the next few steps.)

2. Drain potatoes and press through a ricer into a 4-quart bowl. Sprinkle hot riced potatoes with ¾ teaspoon salt and pepper.

3. Crack egg into a small bowl; whisk lightly. Pour over potato and gently mix by hand until just incorporated.

4. Sprinkle mixture with ½ cup flour and mix by hand just until flour is incorporated. Do not overmix; doing so will make the gnocchi gummy.

5. Divide dough into 4 parts. Using a liberal amount of the remaining flour, roll dough into a ½-inch-diameter rope.

6. Cut gnocchi into 1-inch pieces using a paring knife and dusting the blade with flour as needed to prevent sticking. Handling carefully, place the delicate gnocchi on a baking sheet lined with flour-dusted parchment paper.

7. In an 8-quart stockpot, bring 6 quarts water and 1 tablespoon salt to a boil. Gently tip the parchment paper into the pot, allowing the gnocchi to fall into the water. Remove and discard paper; prepare ice-water bath in a medium bowl.

8. When gnocchi rise to the surface, remove with a slotted spoon and place in ice-water bath. Hold in ice water until gnocchi have stopped cooking and are cold to the touch.

9. Drain gnocchi and lay on a towel to remove excess moisture. Place gnocchi in a dry bowl and toss with canola oil. Pour gnocchi onto a waxed paper–lined baking sheet and freeze until firm. Package in a freezer bag; freeze for up to a couple of months.

BROWN BUTTER GNOCCHI

SERVES 4

BROWN BUTTER SAUCE
4 tablespoons unsalted butter
8 fresh parsley stems and ¼ cup fresh parsley leaves
2 tablespoons minced shallot
1 teaspoon balsamic vinegar
½ teaspoon kosher salt
⅛ teaspoon black pepper

1. Heat butter in a small (1½-quart) heavy saucepan over moderately high heat until foam subsides. Fry parsley stems until crisp, about 3 minutes. Remove and discard stems.

2. Add shallot to butter and cook, stirring, until shallot is golden and butter is deep golden, 1 to 2 minutes. Add balsamic vinegar (butter will foam), then remove from heat. Stir in parsley leaves and season with salt and pepper.

To finish:

3 tablespoons canola oil, divided
1 recipe Gnocchi (p. 69), frozen,
    divided
⅜ teaspoon salt, divided
Freshly ground black pepper
1½ tablespoons butter, divided
¼ teaspoon balsamic vinegar
¼ teaspoon truffle oil
Parmesan cheese

Brown Butter Gnocchi

1. Heat a large sauté pan over very high heat. Working in three batches, begin by heating 1 tablespoon canola oil to smoking point. Add one-third of the Gnocchi and stir until it starts to brown. Add ⅛ teaspoon salt, 1 twist black pepper, and ½ tablespoon butter. Cook until gnocchi are golden brown on the sides; remove gnocchi from pan and hold on a serving plate. Repeat with remaining two batches.

2. Top gnocchi with brown butter sauce and a drizzle of balsamic vinegar and truffle oil. Using a vegetable peeler, shave Parmesan over gnocchi. Finish with freshly ground black pepper. Serve.

LOBSTER GNOCCHI

SERVES 4–6

1 tablespoon canola oil
½ recipe Gnocchi (p. 69), frozen
1 cup roughly chopped lobster meat
½ English cucumber, quartered lengthwise and sliced crosswise to about ¼ inch thick
½ teaspoon thyme leaves
¼ cup heavy cream
½ teaspoon salt
½ cup Lobster Stock (p. 165)
⅛ teaspoon freshly ground black pepper

1. Add canola oil to a large sauté pan on high heat; heat to smoking point and add Gnocchi. Cook, shaking pan occasionally, until nice and brown on the sides, about 4 minutes.

2. Add lobster, cucumber, and thyme and toss to combine; warm through for about 1 minute.

3. Add cream, salt, Lobster Stock, and pepper and reduce to a sauce-like consistency, about 3 minutes. Serve immediately, but only to people who will reciprocate the invitation.

SIDES

CAULIFLOWER FRITTERS

SERVES 4

CHEDDAR SAUCE

2 tablespoons butter

2 tablespoons flour

1 cup skim milk

¾ teaspoon salt

1 cup finely shredded sharp white Cheddar cheese

1. Melt butter in a medium (2-quart) saucepan over medium heat. Add flour and cook 5 minutes over medium to low heat, stirring constantly with a wooden spoon.

2. Add milk and salt to saucepan. Turn heat to high and bring mixture to a boil, stirring constantly. Reduce heat to medium and simmer 8 to 12 minutes, stirring occasionally to prevent burning.

3. Over low heat, add cheese and stir 30 seconds. Remove from heat, cover sauce, and keep warm.

FOR BATTER:

1 egg, separated

⅛ teaspoon salt

1 teaspoon butter, softened

½ cup plus 2 tablespoons all-purpose flour

½ cup water

2 teaspoons brandy

1. Whisk egg white to soft peaks in a 2-quart bowl. Set aside.

2. Whisk together egg yolk, salt, and butter in a separate 2-quart bowl until thick. Whisk about one-third of the flour into the yolk mixture, then whisk in about one-third of the water. Whisk in brandy and continue mixing, adding and alternating water and flour, until fully incorporated. Fold in whipped egg white. Refrigerate until needed.

FOR CAULIFLOWER:

1 tablespoon salt

6 quarts water

1 head cauliflower, cored and broken into 2-inch florets

Bring salt and water to a boil. Add cauliflower and cook until tender, about 5 minutes. Drain cauliflower through strainer; rinse under cold water. Once cool, set aside in refrigerator until ready to fry.

TO FINISH:

3 cups canola oil

Salt

Freshly ground nutmeg

1. Heat oil to 375°F in a small (1½-quart) saucepan. Add blanched cauliflower to batter; mix well.

2. Drop 6 to 8 coated florets into hot oil. Cook until golden brown, about 2 minutes, and remove crisped florets with slotted spoon. Drain on paper towel; immediately sprinkle with a pinch of salt. Repeat with remaining florets.

3. Spoon Cheddar Sauce onto plate. Place florets on top of sauce and, using a microplane, grate nutmeg over cauliflower. Serve immediately.

Cauliflower Fritters

Shefzilla was born from a review of Heidi's in early 2008 by the food critic of the *Star Tribune*, Rick Nelson, in which he wrote, "I have always admired Stewart Woodman's cooking. I was crazy about it at Levain; ditto at the ill-fated Five Restaurant & Street Lounge. Yeah, I'm clued into the guy's Chefzilla reputation, although I've never witnessed it firsthand. But here's the deal: I don't care if Woodman makes the foul-tempered Gordon Ramsay look like Rachael Ray hopped up on happy pills. I eat his food, period. And I feel fortunate when I do, because, trust me, Woodman possesses a prodigious culinary talent."

At first his approach seemed outrageous: he had essentially said, "I have heard this guy is a real jackass. No, I am not going to provide any proof, but why don't you let your imagination run wild, and by the way I still like his work." The sentiment was somewhat a call to arms. I had suddenly been turned into a caricature similar to that of a professional wrestler, one of the "bad guys," a heel.

I knew instantly that we had to lead an exploration into the nature of people's perceptions and projections as they related to me and to food and dining. Heidi and I thought a suitable place for such examination would be a food blog. Early on, the blog focused on industry insider topics. In time, we began to own the Shefzilla persona and to provide a place in the community that was not media-centric, honoring the original intention to learn and share ideas. These days, if something happens in town or around the country, people tune in to get our perception. Isn't technology grand? On the other hand, the blog has done nothing to assuage my "bad boy" image.

WILD RICE AND CREMINI HOT DISH

SERVES 4 AS A SIDE DISH

In Minnesota, the *hot dish* is a staple at family functions, and hot dish and wild rice go together like spam and eggs. This version helpfully balances out a meal that needs something a bit heavier — a hearty vegetarian side to satisfy both the carnivores and the birdseed eaters.

FOR WILD RICE:
¾ cup wild rice
1 teaspoon salt

Place rice and salt in a 4-quart stockpot and cover with 3 quarts water. Bring to a boil; cook 30 minutes, until rice pops open. Strain, then cool rice on a plate. Set aside.

FOR MUSHROOMS:

8 ounces cremini

1 tablespoon canola oil

¼ teaspoon salt

1. Rinse mushrooms quickly in cold water to remove any dirt. Pat dry with a paper towel. Trim stems and quarter mushrooms.

2. Heat a sauté pan on high 3 minutes; add oil, mushrooms, and salt. Cook 5 to 8 minutes, stirring constantly.

3. Add ¼ cup water; deglaze pan and reduce until liquid has evaporated, 3 to 4 minutes. Remove from heat; cool mushrooms on a plate; set aside.

FOR HOT DISH:

2 tablespoons butter

2 tablespoons flour

1 cup skim milk

¾ teaspoon kosher salt

1 cup finely shredded sharp white Cheddar cheese

⅛ teaspoon freshly ground black pepper

1 tablespoon chopped parsley

3 tablespoons panko (Japanese bread crumbs)

1. Preheat oven to 400°F. Melt butter in medium (2-quart) saucepan over medium heat. Add flour and cook 2 minutes, stirring constantly with a wooden spoon.

2. Add milk and salt. Turn heat to high and bring to a boil, stirring constantly. Simmer 8 minutes, stirring occasionally to prevent burning.

3. Reduce heat to low; add cheese, stirring 30 seconds. Add cooked mushrooms, cooked wild rice, pepper, and parsley; stir well to combine.

4. Spoon mixture into oven-safe dish. Top with panko and bake, uncovered, 15 minutes. Serve.

Mini Buttered Potatoes

MINI BUTTERED POTATOES

SERVES 4

I pair this side with Poached Halibut with Roasted Beets and Basil (p. 84), but the flavor profile is a crowd pleaser in any context. It's an easy way to spice up a sometimes boring dish.

1 pound small potatoes
1⅛ teaspoons salt, divided
4 sprigs thyme
½ tablespoon black peppercorns
2 tablespoons butter
⅜ teaspoon ground juniper

1. Halve any potatoes larger than 2 inches and rinse in cold water. Place potatoes in a medium (2-quart) saucepan; add water to cover (about 3½ cups), 1 teaspoon salt, thyme, and black peppercorns. Bring potatoes to a simmer over high heat. Reduce heat to low and cook for 1 hour, until tender.

2. Drain off liquid and cool potatoes 5 minutes. Peel cooked potatoes using tip of a paring knife.

3. Heat butter in small sauté pan over medium heat. Add ground juniper and potatoes, season with ⅛ teaspoon salt, and cook, tossing pan to jostle potatoes for an even, lightly browned finish. Remove from heat. Serve.

CHIVEY POTATO PUREE

SERVES 4

Follow this recipe for a side dish that's creamy, if a bit runny, and meant to be enjoyed with short ribs or bone marrow — or as a meal in itself.

1½ pounds russet potatoes, peeled and cut into eighths
1 teaspoon salt, divided
4 tablespoons heavy cream
1 tablespoon sour cream
⅛ teaspoon freshly ground black pepper
1 tablespoon minced chives
⅛ teaspoon truffle salt

1. Place potatoes, ½ teaspoon salt, and cold water to cover (about 5 cups) in a large saucepan. Bring to a simmer over medium heat and cook for 1 hour.

2. Drain potatoes, reserving about 1 cup water. Combine hot potatoes, heavy cream, and sour cream in bowl of standing mixer fitted with whisk attachment. Mix on low speed 30 seconds. Scrape down sides of bowl.

3. Add ½ teaspoon salt, pepper, and ¼ cup reserved water; mix on high for about 1 minute. Adjust consistency by adding more cooking water if necessary; add chives and truffle salt and mix until just combined. Serve.

Chivey Potato Puree

SWEET AND SPICY TURNIPS

Serves 4

Excellent alongside any beef dish.

2 tablespoons canola oil
2 tablespoons butter
1 pound turnips, peeled, halved, and sliced thin
2 tablespoons Citrus Vinaigrette (p. 151)
½ teaspoon Sriracha
1 teaspoon honey
1½ teaspoons lemon juice
¼ teaspoon salt
1 tablespoon chives

1. Place canola oil in a large sauté pan and heat until smokin' hot. Add butter and turnips; let sit undisturbed to allow turnips to brown, 2 to 3 minutes. Continue cooking, stirring occasionally, about 3 additional minutes.

2. Add Citrus Vinaigrette, Sriracha, honey, lemon juice, and salt. Toss to glaze vegetables, add chives, and serve.

SAUTÉED GREEN BEANS AND PEANUTS

Serves 4

I have to prepare this dish right before I serve it — otherwise it never makes it to the table.

¾ pound green beans, trimmed and cut into 1-inch pieces
2 tablespoons canola oil
¼ cup water
1½ tablespoons finely grated fresh ginger
½ cup roughly chopped Spanish peanuts, toasted and lightly salted
1½ teaspoons sesame oil

¼ teaspoon salt
⅛ teaspoon freshly ground black pepper
Red pepper flakes

1. Bring a large pot of salted water to a boil; cook beans until tender, about 5 minutes. Drain beans and rinse well under cold running water. Pat dry with paper towels.

2. Heat canola oil in a large, heavy skillet over high heat until hot but not smoking. Add green beans and cook and stir until hot; add water and cook, stirring often, until liquid is almost completely evaporated, about 3 to 6 minutes.

3. Add ginger and cook and stir until softened and fragrant, about 30 seconds. Add peanuts and cook and stir 1 minute. Stir in sesame oil, salt, and black and red pepper. Remove from heat.

This dish can be made up to 30 minutes before serving (see above note). Let stand in skillet, uncovered. Reheat over high heat, stirring often, about 2 minutes. Transfer to serving dish and enjoy.

SPRING BEANS AND PEAS

SERVES 4

TO BLANCH:
2 quarts water
1 tablespoon salt
¾ cup green beans
1¾ cups snow peas
6 ounces English peas, shelled to yield about ¼ cup peas

1. Place water and salt in a large saucepan over high heat and bring to a hard boil. Blanch beans 4 to 4½ minutes, until they split easily when pressed. Remove beans and cool under cold running water; drain and split beans lengthwise. Refrigerate until ready to use.

2. Blanch snow peas 2½ minutes. Remove peas and cool under cold running water; drain and refrigerate until ready to use.

3. Blanch English peas 1½ minutes. Remove peas and cool under cold running water; drain and refrigerate until ready to use.

To finish:

¼ cup water

3 tablespoons butter

1½ teaspoons minced lemongrass (remove outer leaves; use bottom 3 inches of stalk)

½ teaspoon salt

Dash cayenne pepper

½ teaspoon dry mustard

1. Place water in a large sauté pan over high heat and bring to a boil. Add butter and whisk to incorporate — you're making a beurre fondue.

2. Add lemongrass, salt, cayenne, and mustard; whisk to blend.

3. Add reserved green beans, snow peas, and English peas. Simmer to reduce most of the liquid, stirring to glaze vegetables. Remove from heat and serve.

SEAFOOD

POACHED HALIBUT WITH ROASTED BEETS AND BASIL

SERVES 4

FOR ROASTED BEETS:
5 (2- to 3-inch diameter) beets
¼ teaspoon kosher salt
⅛ teaspoon black pepper

1. Preheat oven to 400°F. Trim tops and bottoms of beets; peel beets and cut into 1-inch pieces.

2. Place beet pieces on 18-by-12-inch aluminum foil sheet; toss with salt and pepper. Fold foil over beets; seal at top and sides.

3. Set foil package on baking sheet and place in oven. Cook 40 minutes or until beet pieces are tender and easily pierced with a fork. Remove from foil and set aside.

(recipe continues)

Poached Halibut with Roasted Beets and Basil

Preparing halibut

FOR HALIBUT:
1¼ cups Fumet (p. 160)
4 (4- to 6-ounce) skinless halibut fillets
½ teaspoon salt

1. Bring Fumet to a simmer in a pot large enough to hold the halibut. Season halibut fillets equally with salt.

2. Place halibut in fumet presentation side down. Cover pan and cook on medium heat 2 to 3 minutes. Turn each fillet. Reduce heat to low; cook, covered, 3 additional minutes.

3. Check fish for doneness with a toothpick: there should be no resistance in the middle, nor should the fillets be tough. Remove from heat.

PRESENTATION:
½ cup Citrus Vinaigrette (p. 151), divided
½ teaspoon fleur de sel
12 small basil leaves, torn

Chop beets and toss with ¼ cup Citrus Vinaigrette. Divide beets among 4 plates. Drizzle 1 tablespoon vinaigrette around beets. Place poached halibut on top of beets. Sprinkle fleur de sel evenly atop halibut, and garnish with torn basil. Serve.

Let's face it: no one wants their home to smell like a fish market when their guests walk through the door.

Take a couple of steps to combat this problem: the purchase and the rinse.

When buying fish, I usually avoid the supermarket, where staff generally are not all that friendly when you ask if you can smell something. There is nothing more important to buying fish than the smell. If it smells like anything other than the ocean, you don't want it, and neither do your guests. Better to shop at your local fishmonger and insist that he or she let you have a look at the fish you are about to buy. Give it a quick whiff: one smell is enough to tell you it will bode well (sorry, couldn't resist).

Always rinse your "catch." Mix about ½ tablespoon salt with about 6 cups cold water, let it sit, and then stir again. Once the salt appears to be dissolved, lay the fish in the liquid 5 minutes, remove and pat dry, and return to the fridge until you are ready to cook it.

POACHED STRIPED BASS WITH BRAISED CELERY

Serves 4

1 head celery, outermost stalks scrubbed clean and reserved for juicing, innermost stalks reserved
    for braising, inner pale green and yellow leaves picked, rinsed, and reserved for garnish
4 (4- to 6-ounce) portions skinless striped bass
¾ teaspoon salt, divided
1 tablespoon butter
1 cup water
1 bay leaf

1. Process large outer celery stalks in juicer to yield 1 cup juice. Set aside.

2. Peel internal celery stalks and cut into 2½-by-½-inch batons.

3. About 10 minutes before cooking, sprinkle bass portions evenly with ½ teaspoon salt.

4. Melt butter in a medium, flat-sided sauté pan over medium heat. Add celery batons and ⅛
    teaspoon salt and sweat over low heat about 10 minutes.

5. Add water and reduce by half over medium heat. Add reserved celery juice and bay leaf; cook
    over high heat 15 minutes, stirring occasionally.

6. Add bass to pan, presentation side down, reduce heat to medium, and cook 3 minutes. Using
    a slotted spatula, turn fish over and cook an additional 2 to 3 minutes. Remove bass with a
    slotted spatula; place each piece in the center of 4 serving bowls.

7. Add ⅛ teaspoon salt to celery and broth mixture and reduce over medium heat 2 to 4 min-
    utes. Divide celery batons and broth among the 4 bowls, topping the bass and finishing with
    reserved celery leaves. Serve.

MARINATED AND STEAMED TILAPIA WITH ROSEMARY PILAF

SERVES 4

Tilapia is a vegetarian fish, making it much easier to farm raise and less hard on the environment than some other fish. Steam this feel-good ingredient for a real treat.

ROSEMARY PILAF

2 tablespoons extra-virgin olive oil
1 cup finely chopped onion
2 inches rosemary stem, leaves attached
1 cup long-grain white rice
1¼ teaspoons salt
1¾ cups water

1. Heat oil in large saucepan on medium heat. Add onions and sweat until translucent, stirring occasionally, 8 to 9 minutes.

Steamed Tilapia

2. Add rosemary and stir. Quickly add remaining ingredients (rice through water). Stir once and bring to a boil. Cover pot with a tight-fitting lid and reduce heat to low. Simmer about 20 minutes, until liquid is absorbed.

3. Remove from heat and allow to stand, covered and undisturbed, another 10 to 15 minutes. Fluff rice with a fork and discard rosemary.

FOR MARINATED TILAPIA:

2 tablespoons olive oil

Zest and 1½ teaspoons juice from 1 lemon

Zest and 2 tablespoons juice from 1 orange

1 teaspoon chopped fresh thyme

½ teaspoon salt

1½ to 2 pounds tilapia

1. Whisk together olive oil, zests and juices, thyme, and salt in a medium bowl. Add fish and marinate, refrigerated, 15 minutes. Meanwhile, preheat grill.

2. Remove fish from marinade and place on 16-by-16-inch piece of aluminum foil. Fold up sides of foil to create a bowl and pour in marinade. Seal package by rolling together opposite sides of foil.

3. Place fish on hot grill; cover and cook 10 minutes. Remove from grill and serve immediately with pilaf.

BROILED SALMON WITH PICKLED SHALLOT BEURRE BLANC

SERVES 8–10

FOR SALMON:

1 side of salmon (2½ to 3 pounds), pin bones removed

2 teaspoons salt

¼ teaspoon freshly ground black pepper

2 egg yolks, lightly beaten

1. Place oven rack 5 to 6 inches away from broiler; preheat broiler. Line baking sheet with aluminum foil.

2. Prepare the salmon by removing the skin in one piece; do not discard. Season both sides of the skinless fillet with salt and pepper. Reassemble the salmon — place the fillet back on the skin — and place skin side down on the baking sheet.

3. Coat salmon evenly with beaten yolks using a pastry brush.

4. Broil salmon 10 minutes or until desired doneness. Rotate pan often during cooking for even browning. Allow to rest 5 minutes.

Pickled Shallot Beurre Blanc
⅔ cup liquid and shallots from Pickled Shallots (p. 157)
½ cup (1 stick) butter

1. Place pickling liquid and shallots in a small saucepan, turn heat to high, and bring to a boil. Reduce heat to medium, add butter, and whisk vigorously until incorporated, 2 to 3 minutes.

2. Remove from heat and transfer sauce to another pot so that it doesn't overheat and break down; keep warm until ready to serve. The sauce can be served shallots and all, but for a smoother texture, pour through a fine-mesh strainer and discard solids.

Presentation:
This dish — easy to serve because the skin has already been separated from the fillet — is perfect for a family-style supper or a buffet. Transfer the fish on the foil onto a serving platter for a rustic look and pour sauce over salmon. The sauce and the broiled yolk coating work wonderfully together.

TUNA BURGER ON DOUBLE SESAME BUN WITH SLAW

Serves 8

Double Sesame Bun
1 cup lukewarm water
2 tablespoons sesame oil

Cooks differ from foodies in a significant way: first and foremost, they love not just to eat but to cook as well. Foodies love to eat; they may have dined at some of the world's great restaurants and have extraordinarily refined palates. But the little old lady who cooks, who stands over the stove for the sheer joy of it, who never traveled a lick and never ate at the great restaurants — she knows as much or more about food than the most well-traveled foodie ever will.

The result of this cultural divide is significant. The foodie in me tends toward wanting to consume the latest trend or fad, while the cook in me simply wants to eat good food. Simple or complicated, whatever it is must be executed properly. If done correctly, cooks will follow you into a hail of bullets, but if they sense laziness, watch out. If cooks think you are praying at the altar of fame and fortune, that you have abandoned the religion, they take no prisoners. I have been berated by cooks who thought I had not done something right, but the feeling of fidelity that comes when a cook compliments your work is beyond measure.

Cooking is magical on many levels. The cook's primary experience — watching an ingredient transform into something different right before his or her eyes — never gets old. In fact, just the opposite is true: with every risotto, with every dish I cook, I fall more deeply in love with the craft. It's alchemy, and every cook shares the basic need to try to create gold from lead. Foodies may laud the result, but only cooks can truly appreciate what it took to achieve it.

1 large egg
3½ cups all-purpose flour
¼ cup sugar
1¼ teaspoons salt
1 tablespoon instant yeast
3 tablespoons black sesame seeds

1. Combine first 7 ingredients (water through yeast) in bowl of a standing mixer fitted with dough hook; knead until glossy, about 7 minutes. Transfer dough to large greased bowl, cover, and let rise 1 hour, or until doubled.

2. Gently deflate dough and divide into 8 pieces. Shape each piece into a round 1 inch thick; flatten to about 3 inches across. Place buns on lightly greased or parchment paper–lined baking sheet, and let rise, uncovered, about 1 hour, until very puffy.

3. Preheat oven to 375°F. If desired, brush buns with melted butter or with egg wash (1 egg beaten with 1 tablespoon water), and sprinkle with sesame seeds. Bake buns 10 to 15 minutes, until golden. Cool on a rack.

SPICY MAYO

¼ cup Mayonnaise (p. 169)

1 teaspoon Sriracha

Stir together Mayonnaise and Sriracha; refrigerate until ready to use.

SLAW

2 cups red cabbage, cut into julienne strips

2 cups jicama, cut into julienne strips

2 cups Dipping Sauce (p. 152)

2 teaspoons lime juice

Stir together all ingredients in a large bowl. Cover and refrigerate 2 hours.

Tuna Burger on Double Sesame Bun with Slaw

FOR TUNA BURGER:

1 pound coarse-ground tuna

4 teaspoons Dijon-style mustard

2 teaspoons dry mustard

1 teaspoon sugar

1 egg

1. Stir together all ingredients in a medium bowl. Form mixture into 8 equal patties, each about 1 inch thick. Cover a plate with plastic wrap, place patties on top of plastic wrap, cover with additional plastic wrap, and refrigerate 30 minutes.

2. Preheat grill; cook patties 2 minutes on each side. Remove from heat.

PRESENTATION:

Slice buns, spread Spicy Mayo on bun halves, add burger, and top with Slaw. Serve.

SEARED SCALLOPS AND ARTICHOKES WITH CARROT CURRY

SERVES 4

This recipe is like me: complicated on the surface but—once you delve a little deeper—shockingly simple.

FOR ARTICHOKES:
Juice of 1 lemon
4 medium (4- to 5-inch diameter) artichokes
1 cup canola oil
1 cup extra-virgin olive oil
⅛ teaspoon red pepper flakes
1 clove garlic, thinly sliced
2 sprigs thyme
⅛ teaspoon salt

1. Fill a large bowl with 3 quarts cold water and lemon juice.

2. Trim the outside of each artichoke with a serrated knife until the tender leaves are revealed and choke is visible. Discard outer leaves. Trim top of artichoke down to fuzzy choke, dipping frequently into lemon water to prevent browning. Use tip of small spoon to remove and discard the fuzzy choke.

3. Cut artichoke hearts into eighths; place in lemon water and set aside.

4. Stir together canola and olive oils, red pepper flakes, garlic, thyme, and salt in a large (4-quart) saucepan over medium heat. Add artichoke hearts and cook 6 to 7 minutes. Remove from heat.

5. Strain artichokes, reserving oil, and set aside. Set aside 2 tablespoons oil for scallops; reserve remainder, refrigerated, for later use in vinaigrettes and dressings.

(recipe continues)

Peeling an artichoke

CARROT CURRY SAUCE

1½ teaspoons plus 6 tablespoons butter, divided
½ medium shallot, sliced
Pinch salt
Up to 1½ teaspoons Curry Powder (p. 155), to taste
½ cup chardonnay
¾ cup carrot juice
⅛ teaspoon cayenne pepper
1½ teaspoons lime juice

1. Stir together 1½ teaspoons butter, shallot, and salt in medium saucepan over medium-low heat. Sweat 5 minutes, until shallot is translucent.

2. Add Curry Powder; toss in pan 30 seconds to lightly brown. Add chardonnay and reduce 5 minutes. Increase heat to medium for a hard simmer; add carrot juice and reduce mixture to ½ to ⅓ cup. Remove from heat.

3. Place mixture in container of electric blender; cover and blend 1 minute. Return to pan and return to boil. Whisk in 6 tablespoons butter and add cayenne and lime juice. Remove from pan and keep warm until ready to serve.

FOR SCALLOPS:

8 large (U10) scallops
½ teaspoon salt
¼ teaspoon black pepper
2 tablespoons artichoke oil

1. Season scallops with salt and pepper.

2. Place 1 tablespoon oil in a small sauté pan set over high heat and bring to smoking point. Add 4 scallops and cook 2 minutes, until browned on top. Turn over scallops for a moment and then immediately remove from pan. Repeat with remaining oil and scallops.

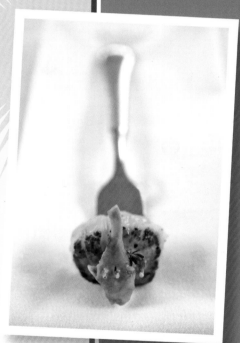

Seared Scallops and Artichokes with Carrot Currey

PRESENTATION:

Divide artichokes among 4 plates. Halve scallops along the equator to create two disks and place atop artichokes. Pour sauce around plate. Serve.

The key — and now here is the skinny, the low down, and, no, it's not "fried monkey's butt," as Heidi likes to call it — that makes for great food is, drum roll, please: fresh ingredients.

People often ask how I managed to make something taste so good: what is the secret? Much of the time it comes down to cooking fresh ingredients. As an example, imagine if you will scallops that came to the line at Le Bernardin still pulsating, having just been taken from their shells. Rinsed briefly and laid in a pan, they required little more than slight seasoning to be properly cooked. The freshness of eating a scallop thus prepared cannot be overstated: it's one of the reasons Le Bernardin continues to be one of the world's great seafood restaurants.

What can we home cooks do? How do we ensure freshness? It's quite simple: cook the way they did in the old country. The items you buy in large batches should be prepped in large batches for preserving, but otherwise shop small. Keep the rotation of your fruits, vegetables, and proteins to within a couple three days; plan and shop accordingly. Tuck into the market for a minute or two, make a beeline for the few items you need, and steal back into the night.

FRIED TROUT AND REFRIGERATOR PICKLES

SERVES 4

REFRIGERATOR PICKLES

1 English cucumber
1 teaspoon mustard seed, toasted
1 teaspoon cumin seeds, toasted and ground
1 bay leaf
1 teaspoon salt
½ cup rice wine vinegar
3 teaspoons sugar
1 clove garlic, thinly sliced

1. Rinse cucumber and, using a mandolin, slice very thin, into ⅛-inch rounds. Place in stainless mixing bowl.

2. Preheat small saucepan over medium heat. Add remaining ingredients (mustard seed through garlic) to pan and cook until mixture begins to simmer and sugar dissolves, about 3 minutes. Continue cooking 1 additional minute, until garlic is soft. Remove from heat.

3. Pour liquid over cucumbers and toss to evenly coat. Refrigerate to chill before serving.

FOR TROUT:

½ cup matzo meal
¼ cup all-purpose flour
1 tablespoon salt
½ teaspoon freshly ground black pepper
2 egg whites
⅓ cup milk
2 tablespoons High Heel Honey (made by my in-laws; substitute other honey as desired)
2 whole trout, scaled, split, heads and pin bones removed (or 4 skin-on trout fillets)
2 tablespoons butter, divided
2 tablespoons canola oil, divided
1 tablespoon lemon juice

Removing pin bones

1. Mix together matzo meal, flour, salt, and pepper in a medium bowl.

2. Mix together egg whites, milk, and honey in a separate bowl.

3. Dip trout halves or fillets in milk mixture and then into matzo mixture. Set aside on plate.

4. Melt 1 tablespoon butter and 1 tablespoon oil in a large sauté pan over high heat, bringing nearly to the smoking point.

5. Add 2 pieces trout and cook over medium to high heat until golden brown on both sides, about 5 minutes total. Add ½ tablespoon lemon juice, baste fish with pan juices, and remove from pan. Repeat with remaining ingredients. Serve immediately with pickles.

There's a John Lennon song, "Working Class Hero," that includes the line, "giving you no time instead of it all." Through his lyrics, Lennon addresses the overarching tendency for us to apply rules to everything. That's why I love the tune: "they" give us a lot of "shoulds" in our lives. When it comes to cooking at home, keep one thing in mind: Jean-Georges cooked his risotto — for example — in an entirely different way than did Ripert, Ducasse, Romano, or Kunz. Don't worry so much about making it the right way. If you like some aspect of a recipe, add it to another; tweak and play as you go. The results will not only be satisfying, they will also be personal — they will be you.

All too often we assume there must be a right way to do things: a right way to do a sit-up, to mow the lawn, to talk to your kid. As I get a little longer in the tooth and wider in the midsection, my philosophy regarding perfection seems to be morphing. Yes, you have only one life to live, and by George if that shouldn't be a fight to the death, I don't know what should. But in cooking and in life, worrying about doing things the right way too often gets in the way of doing anything at all.

Don't let the perfect be the enemy of the good, as they say. Between you and me, when you cook for your family, the result is sometimes going to be ignored, no matter how good or bad it is. Remember, they can't choose a different restaurant tomorrow night. Even if they did, nothing that is prepared by hand with love in your home can compare.

Fried Trout and
Refrigerator Pickles

BIRDS

MARINATED AND GRILLED CORNISH HENS WITH ROAST ONION RISOTTO

SERVES 4

For the garnish, brown the onions reserved from the marinade nice and slow in a cast-iron skillet.

FOR HENS:

2 (1½-pound) Cornish hens
1 medium onion, thinly sliced
5 cloves garlic, thinly sliced
¼ cup extra-virgin olive oil
2 teaspoons salt
¼ teaspoon black pepper

Marinated and Grilled Cornish Hens with Roast Onion Risotto

1. Place whole Cornish hen breast side down with drumsticks pointing toward you. The backbone is now on top, running down the center of the bird. Hold the tail and use a kitchen shears along each side of the backbone, cutting all the way through, from end to end, to remove the entire backbone.

2. Place the hen skin side down and with a knife cut the cartilage covering the breastbone, splitting the hen in two. Repeat with second bird.

3. Place all 4 pieces in a large bowl; add remaining ingredients (onion through pepper) and mix to evenly distribute the marinade. Cover and refrigerate up to 6 hours.

ROAST ONION RISOTTO

This technique was discovered when I accidentally left the onions on for too long. The results, however, had Heidi looking at me with a certain gleam in her eyes. The key to creamy texture: stir the rice constantly as it absorbs the water.

4 cups water
3 tablespoons butter
1 medium onion, minced
1 cup Arborio rice
1 cup white wine
1¼ teaspoons salt
⅛ teaspoon black pepper
⅔ cup grated Parmesan-Reggiano or Pecorino-Romano cheese

1. Bring water to a simmer in a large saucepan. Preheat a wide-rimmed, high-sided pan over medium heat; melt butter.

2. Add onion, reduce heat to low, and cook 30 to 40 minutes, until dark brown. Add rice, turn heat to medium, and stir 7 minutes to toast. Add wine, salt, and pepper and cook, stirring, over medium heat until rice is almost dry.

3. Add 1 cup simmering water; stirring constantly, cook until rice has absorbed all liquid. Repeat, 1 cup at a time, until all the water has been added, about 25 minutes, and rice is tender but not mushy.

4. Fold in grated cheese. Serve immediately with the hens, or serve as a summer entrée with a little salad.

TO COOK THE HENS:

1. Preheat grill to medium. Remove hens from oil; remove onion and garlic from hens and oil; discard oil.

2. Slowly cook the onions and garlic in a cast-iron skillet over low to medium heat until golden brown and soft. Set aside.

3. Place hens skin side up on grill and cook 10 to 15 minutes; flip to skin side down and grill an additional 15 minutes. Check thigh joint to ensure proper doneness: there should be no pink at the bone. Remove hens from grill and let rest 5 minutes.

Place risotto in a bowl and stack chicken on a platter. Top with caramelized onions and garlic. Serve.

At the idea that "water is the enemy of great food" most people might scoff. After all, water is the building block of life.

All too often cooks view water as having a neutral effect, a most common mistake. When not used properly, water leeches away flavor, color, and valuable nutrients. It's hardly benign. The best example is when blanching vegetables: the quicker you have them in and out of the water, the better. Use a large enough volume of blanching water, and cook in small batches. Likewise, the quicker you "shock" them (plunge in ice water to stop the cooking process) and remove them from the shocking water, the better.

In other words, view water with more suspicion than you usually do. Consider it a tool — and treat it as you would any other. Leaving something in water is no different than leaving it in the oven for too long. More time does not necessarily equal better flavor. Think of water as a benevolent friend: pleasantly disposed, not hostile, but powerful nonetheless.

GRILLED DUCK WITH VERMICELLI AND FRESH HERBS

SERVES 4

SESAME PEANUT PASTE
1 teaspoon freshly grated ginger
¼ cup chopped crystallized ginger
1 teaspoon minced garlic
1 Thai chili pepper
5 teaspoons sugar
⅛ teaspoon salt

½ cup unsalted peanuts, toasted and cooled
6 tablespoons white sesame seeds, toasted
¼ cup sesame oil
¼ cup peanut oil

1. Combine both gingers, garlic, chili, sugar, salt, and 2 tablespoons water in container of electric blender; cover and process for 1 minute.

2. Add peanuts, sesame seeds, and ½ cup water; blend for 2 minutes.

3. Add another ½ cup water and blend for a few seconds. With blender running, slowly add sesame and peanut oils. Set aside ¼ cup of mixture; reserve remainder, refrigerated, for future use.

Grilled Duck with
Vermicelli and Fresh Herbs

FOR VERMICELLI:
1 cup loosely packed fresh mint leaves, rinsed
4 ounces bean thread vermicelli
1 tablespoon sesame oil

1. Bring 3 quarts water and 1 tablespoon salt to a boil in a large saucepan. Blanch mint leaves 5 seconds. Remove leaves, reserving blanching water to cook vermicelli. Rinse mint under cold water until cool. Set aside for Mint Oil (p. 159).

2. Place dry noodles in a large bowl and pour over enough boiling "mint" water to cover. Let steep 8 to 10 minutes. Drain noodles and rinse 4 minutes, until cold.

3. Shake noodles to remove excess water; toss with sesame oil. Refrigerate until ready to use.

FOR DUCK:
2 (6-ounce) skinless duck breasts
¼ teaspoon salt
¼ teaspoon freshly ground black pepper

1. Preheat grill. Cover breast with plastic wrap and pound to ¼ inch thick. Season thoroughly with salt and pepper.

2. Over a very hot grill, cook duck for 1 minute on each side. Remove to plate; allow to rest 5 minutes, then slice lengthwise.

TO FINISH:
24 cilantro leaves
10 mint leaves, torn into ¼-inch pieces
¼ cup sesame peanut paste
2 teaspoons Sriracha
2 tablespoons rice vinegar
¼ cup water
½ teaspoon salt
12 chives, cut into 2-inch batons
Mint Oil (p. 159)

In large bowl, toss together first 8 ingredients (cilantro through chives) with vermicelli. Divide among 4 plates. Top with sliced duck. Drizzle plates with Mint Oil to garnish. Serve.

POACHED CHICKEN AND WILTED ARUGULA WITH ORZO

SERVES 4

PARSLEY ORZO

1 cup orzo

2 tablespoons butter

4 cloves garlic, thinly sliced

⅜ teaspoon salt

3 tablespoons extra-virgin olive oil

40 threads saffron

⅓ cup chopped fresh parsley

¼ teaspoon black pepper

⅛ teaspoon red pepper flakes

1. Bring 2½ quarts water and 1 teaspoon salt to a boil over high heat. Add orzo and cook, stirring occasionally, 9 minutes. Remove from heat. Drain orzo through strainer and rinse under cold water to stop cooking.

2. Melt butter in a sauté pan over medium heat. Add garlic; sweat 2 minutes, stirring constantly. Butter should be frothy. Remove from pan.

3. In medium bowl, combine garlic and cooked orzo with remaining ingredients (salt through red pepper flakes). Mix well; set aside to macerate 40 minutes.

FOR CHICKEN:

2 cups water

3 tablespoons extra-virgin olive oil

½ tablespoon salt

20 sprigs thyme

¼ teaspoon freshly ground black pepper

1 pound (3 to 4) boneless, skinless chicken breasts

1. Stir together first 5 ingredients (water through pepper) in a medium saucepan over high heat; bring to a simmer.

2. Place chicken in poaching liquid presentation side down; reduce heat to low. Cook 10 minutes, turn chicken, and cook an additional 10 minutes.

3. Remove from heat; hold chicken in poaching liquid 5 minutes. Remove chicken from liquid, rest 8 minutes, and slice before serving.

For arugula:

4 tablespoons butter

6 cloves garlic, thinly sliced

10 ounces baby arugula, rinsed

⅜ teaspoon salt

Extra-virgin olive oil to finish, if desired

1. Melt butter in a large sauté pan over medium heat. Add garlic; sweat 2 to 4 minutes, until slightly brown, stirring constantly. Butter should be frothy.

2. Add arugula and salt; cook 2 to 3 minutes, until lettuce is wilted and most of the liquid has evaporated. Remove from heat.

To finish:

Divide wilted arugula among 4 plates, add a scoop of orzo to each, and arrange sliced chicken on top. Drizzle with good extra-virgin olive oil if desired. Serve.

Juice: it's not just for breakfast anymore. You can cook with it, too — and you should.

Years ago while preparing a large batch of risotto on the line at Union Square Cafe, I had an "aha" moment. The recipe called for substituting squash juice for stock. From that point on, the idea of juicing captured my imagination. Not always for the best, it's true, but so much so that I recommend you also give it a try.

If you don't have a juicer, look no further than your local health-food store; the hippies have long been sticking things in their juicers (I say this as the proud son of hippies). You can also use unsweetened juices from the dry-goods shelf in your supermarket. My favorite item to cook with juice, especially at first, is couscous, a dish that's painfully easy to prepare but often equally as boring. Simply adding vegetable juice makes a delicious difference.

CHICKEN WITH BACON, CAULIFLOWER COUSCOUS, AND KIMCHI

SERVES 4

Blended spicy cabbage sauce with bacon-wrapped chicken: "weird," you say. Yes, but with the added attraction of being very good.

FOR CHICKEN:
4 (6-ounce) boneless, skinless chicken breasts
16 slices bacon
1 tablespoon canola oil

1. Wrap each chicken breast with 3 to 4 slices bacon, pulling bacon tight and overlapping slices by half an inch. Refrigerate until ready to cook. Prepare bok choy and couscous.

2. Preheat oven to 375°F. Heat canola oil in medium sauté pan and brown bacon-wrapped chicken on all sides, beginning with the overlapped side so that bacon seals.

3. Remove chicken from pan and place on a baking sheet; bake 12 minutes or until done. Tent with aluminum foil and rest 8 minutes.

FOR BRAISED BOK CHOY:
¾ pound baby bok choy
1 tablespoon canola oil

1. Slice bok choy in half lengthwise and soak in cold water about 20 minutes, cleaning thoroughly.

2. Bring a pot of salted water to a boil and blanch bok choy about 3 minutes. Strain and run under cold water until cool enough to handle. Pat dry.

3. Heat a sauté pan over medium-high heat, add oil and then bok choy, cut side down. Cook until browned, about 4 minutes. Remove from heat.

(recipe continues)

KIMCHI SAUCE

1 cup white wine

1 shallot, peeled and chopped

½ cup heavy cream

½ cup kimchi, lightly chopped

¼ teaspoon salt

1. Combine wine and shallot in a small (1-quart) saucepan over medium heat and reduce to about 1 tablespoon of liquid.

2. Add cream, kimchi, and salt. Bring to a boil and remove from heat. Puree sauce in blender for 1 minute. Set aside.

Chicken with Bacon, Cauliflower Couscous, and Kimchi

Cauliflower Couscous

½ head cauliflower
1 teaspoon canola oil
7 green onions, whites and greens thinly sliced
¼ teaspoon salt
¼ cup water
⅔ cup couscous

1. Process cauliflower in juicer to yield 1 cup juice.

2. Add canola oil, green onions, and salt to a saucepan over high heat. Cook and stir until lightly browned, about 3 minutes.

3. Add cauliflower juice and water to saucepan and bring to a boil. Remove from heat. Add couscous and let stand, covered, 10 minutes.

Presentation:

Slice the chicken crossways into thin "coins." Arrange in a line. Spoon couscous alongside, drizzle Kimchi Sauce around, and add bok choy. Use ample sauce: the couscous will act as a sponge.

SWEET AND SOUR QUAIL WITH QUICK PICKLED EGGPLANT

Serves 4

Eggplant is not my favorite, generally speaking, but this particular preparation was inspired by a terrific cook and friend, Zehorit. The ingredient combination imparts a complicated flavor profile she learned from her Yemeni parents.

Quick Pickled Eggplant

1 pound eggplant, peeled and sliced into ¾-inch rounds
⅓ cup all-purpose flour
½ cup canola oil
2 teaspoons cumin seeds
⅛ teaspoon cayenne pepper

2 tablespoons sherry vinegar
½ teaspoon salt
1 tablespoon extra-virgin olive oil

1. Toss eggplant in flour to evenly coat. Heat a high-sided sauté pan over medium-high heat. Add oil and cook eggplant slices, stirring, until golden brown, about 5 to 6 minutes per side. The eggplant will be very soft: carefully transfer it to a container that allows all pieces to lie flat.

2. Toast cumin in a small sauté pan on high heat; remove from heat and finely grind in a spice grinder. Stir together with cayenne, vinegar, salt, and olive oil and pour over eggplant, turning to coat. Cover and refrigerate at least 2 hours and up to 1 week.

FOR HONEY SAUCE:
3 tablespoons honey
1 teaspoon fish sauce
½ teaspoon Sriracha

Combine all ingredients in a bowl and mix well. Set aside.

FOR QUAIL:
6 (4- to 5-ounce) quail (up to 2 pounds total)
2 to 3 cups milk
3 cups canola oil

1. Cut along sides of each quail's backbone using a kitchen shears. Remove and discard backbone. Place quail in a large bowl, cover with milk, and refrigerate at least 3 hours.

2. Heat canola oil to 250°F in a large (4-quart) saucepan. Remove quail from milk and pat dry. Discard milk.

3. Place 2 quail in the oil breast side down; adjust heat to maintain a temperature of 250–60°F, and cook about 3 minutes, until golden brown. Turn and cook an additional 3 minutes. Remove quail from oil and set aside. Repeat with remaining quail.

PRESENTATION:
Divide quail among 4 plates. Drizzle with honey sauce and serve with pickled eggplant.

CHICKEN CONFIT WITH COOL YUKON WHIPPED-CREAM POTATOES

SERVES 4–6

FOR CONFIT:

2 pounds (about 6) chicken thighs
1 tablespoon salt
1 bay leaf
1 teaspoon pink peppercorns
3 cups canola oil

1. Sprinkle chicken evenly with salt and add bay leaf and peppercorns. Refrigerate, covered, 12 hours.

2. Rinse chicken and pat dry with paper towels. Place chicken in a slow cooker and cover with canola oil. Cook on low heat 3 hours. Then increase setting to warm and continue to cook for 1½ hours.

3. Store chicken in oil, refrigerated, until ready to serve, up to 2 days.

COOL YUKON WHIPPED-CREAM POTATOES

1 pound Yukon potatoes, scrubbed clean and cut into 1-inch cubes
1½ teaspoons salt, divided
½ cup heavy cream
¼ teaspoon lemon zest
1 teaspoon minced tarragon
¼ teaspoon black pepper
¼ teaspoon dry mustard
1 teaspoon warm water

1. Place potatoes in a large saucepan and add just enough cold water to cover and 1 teaspoon salt. Bring to a boil; reduce heat and simmer 15 to 20 minutes, until tender. Drain potatoes and refrigerate until cool, about 15 minutes.

2. Whip cream to medium peaks; refrigerate.

3. Place chilled potatoes in a large bowl and add whipped cream, lemon zest, tarragon, ½ teaspoon salt, pepper, and dry mustard. Mix together, adding water as needed to adjust consistency. Refrigerate.

(recipe continues)

TO FINISH:
Preheat oven to 425°F. Place chicken skin side up in an oven-safe sauté pan. Bake 15 to 20 minutes, until skin is crisp and golden brown. Serve alongside potato salad.

MEAT

GRILLED LAMB CHOPS WITH YOGURT-CILANTRO SAUCE

FOR LAMB:

2 lamb racks (7 to 8 bones each)

8 cloves garlic, peeled and thinly sliced

1 teaspoon kosher salt

¼ teaspoon black peppercorns, freshly cracked

1½ teaspoons extra-virgin olive oil

6 parsley sprigs, roughly chopped

1. A full lamb rack contains 8 ribs. Slide a knife between each rib and slice into chops, careful to divide meat equally among the chops. Toss chops with garlic, salt, pepper, olive oil, and parsley.

2. Place on large plate and refrigerate 2 to 6 hours.

(recipe continues)

Grilled Lamb Chops with Yogurt-Cilantro Sauce

YOGURT-CILANTRO SAUCE

1 bunch cilantro, rinsed well

1½ teaspoons fennel seed

1 teaspoon cumin seed

¾ teaspoon mustard seed

¼ teaspoon red pepper flakes

1 teaspoon fenugreek

Pinch turmeric powder

2 teaspoons minced garlic

2 teaspoons freshly minced ginger

2 onions, sliced

1 tablespoon plus ½ cup canola oil, divided

2 teaspoons salt

¾ cup plain yogurt

1. Bring pot of water to a boil; blanch cilantro 1 minute. Remove and plunge into cold water, squeeze dry, and chop. Set aside.

2. Toast the dry spices (fennel through turmeric) in a medium sauté pan on high heat; remove from heat and finely grind mixture in a spice grinder. Set aside.

3. Heat 1 tablespoon canola oil in a large sauté pan over medium heat. Sweat garlic, ginger, and onion 8 to 10 minutes. Remove from heat and cool.

4. Combine spices, onion mixture, cilantro, salt, and yogurt in container of an electric blender. Cover and blend until smooth, about 3 minutes. Add ½ cup canola oil; blend 20 seconds more. Set aside.

TO COOK LAMB AND FINISH:

1. Preheat grill. Remove garlic and parsley from lamb. Grill chops to desired doneness (about 2 to 3 minutes per side for medium rare).

2. Serve family style, with cilantro sauce on the side.

One of the biggest shocks when I began cooking at home was discovering how easily distractions can pile up, so much so that the task of cooking seems untenable. It turns into just another chore.

Do yourself a monster favor: buy a few timers. These days they come in all shapes and sizes — small enough to put in your pocket, on a lanyard to wear around your neck. Using them will make your life so much easier. I was careful to add cooking times to these recipes so that you can be mobile while you cook. The idea that you need to stand by for every step of a recipe is just not realistic for most people. True, nothing is exact. Your stove and cookware are particular to your kitchen. You'll have to keep an eye on things, but don't let that stop you from fitting in a load of laundry or tossing your kid on your knee.

LEG OF LAMB AND RANCH SALAD WITH HOME FRIES

SERVES 4–6

I developed this recipe to bring a little more lamb into the menu rotation. The kids love this rendition, especially served with home fries and my creamy ranch-style dressing. Order the long peppers online.

FOR LAMB:

6 long peppers, whole
2 tablespoons fennel seeds
1 teaspoon cumin seeds
2 teaspoons celery salt
1¾ to 2 pounds boneless leg of lamb
½ teaspoon salt

1. Toast long peppers, fennel, and cumin in a sauté pan 1 minute over high heat. Remove to spice grinder, add celery salt, and grind fine.

2. Rub entire surface of lamb evenly with spice mix. Refrigerate lamb for 1 hour and then season with salt. Preheat oven to 500°F.

3. Place rubbed lamb on an aluminum foil–lined baking sheet. Bake 20 minutes.

4. Reduce oven temperature to 200°F and bake lamb an additional 15 minutes. Remove from oven, cover with foil, and let rest 20 minutes before slicing.

HOME FRIES

2 medium russet
  potatoes, scrubbed
  and cut into eighths
  lengthwise

1 tablespoon canola oil

2 tablespoons Chip Mix
  (p. 156)

1. Preheat oven to 350°F.
   Toss potatoes with
   oil and Chip Mix in a
   large bowl.

2. Place potatoes on
   aluminum foil– or
   parchment paper–
   lined baking sheet.
   Bake 20 minutes; flip
   potatoes and bake
   another 10 minutes.
   Set aside.

RANCH-STYLE DRESSING

It's not ranch in the traditional sense, but here's the deal: after awhile, the bottled stuff becomes boring. Try this one on your family members: chances are they will like it better. You can order truffle salt online: it's great to have around.

2 tablespoons water
2 tablespoons sour cream
2 tablespoons Mayonnaise (p. 169)
1 teaspoon lemon juice
⅛ teaspoon truffle salt
¼ teaspoon salt
½ teaspoon crushed fresh green peppercorns

Combine all ingredients in a large mixing bowl; mix well.

To FINISH:

1 head iceberg lettuce, chopped into 2-inch pieces

Add lettuce to dressing mixture and toss. Serve with lamb and Home Fries.

GRILLED STRIP STEAK WITH BRAISED GREENS

Serves 4

BRAISED DINO KALE

2 tablespoons canola oil
3 cloves garlic, thinly sliced
1 bunch dino kale, stemmed and rinsed
½ teaspoon salt
1½ cups water

1. Combine oil and garlic in a large (3-quart) saucepan over medium heat and sweat 1 minute. Add kale to pan; cook and stir 2 minutes; add salt.

2. Add water to pan; bring to a boil and cover. Turn heat to low and cook about 30 minutes, until liquid measures ¼ cup. If necessary, increase heat to reduce. Remove from heat.

FOR STEAK:

2 (12-ounce) strip steaks
1 tablespoon salt
Freshly ground black pepper

1. Cover steaks evenly and completely with salt. Let set on plate at room temperature 10 minutes. Preheat grill.

2. Rinse steaks under cold water to remove salt; pat dry. Season each side with 3 cracks of black pepper.

3. Grill 3 minutes on each side for medium rare. (Cook longer at a lower temperature for a higher degree of doneness.) Remove steaks to a plate and rest 8 minutes before slicing.

PRESENTATION:
Plate braised greens and sliced steak together; use kale cooking liquid as a light sauce. Serve.

SLOW COOKER RIBS

SERVES 4–6

Excellent paired with Chivey Potato Puree (p. 79).

2½ pounds beef chuck boneless "country-style ribs"
¾ teaspoon salt
1 teaspoon pepper
3 tablespoons canola oil, divided
5 shallots, roughly chopped
5 cloves garlic, roughly chopped
2 medium carrots, finely chopped
2 medium onions, finely chopped
3 ribs celery, finely chopped
½ bottle last night's leftover red wine (assuming there is any)
3 sprigs thyme
2 bay leaves
1 bunch parsley stems, tied together with twine
About 4 cups Beef Stock (p. 163), hot
¾ teaspoon fleur de sel or ¼ teaspoon truffle salt

1. Season ribs with salt and pepper. Heat a sauté pan large enough to hold the short ribs in one layer on high heat, add 1 tablespoon canola oil, and brown half of the short ribs on all sides, about 8 minutes total, transferring to a bowl when done. Repeat with 1 tablespoon oil and remaining ribs.

2. Reduce heat to medium. Heat 1 tablespoon canola oil and add vegetables (shallots through celery) to pan and cook, stirring frequently, until softened, about 8 to 12 minutes. Remove from heat and place vegetables in slow cooker.

3. Using the same sauté pan, reduce wine by half over medium heat.

4. Arrange short ribs over vegetables, add reduced wine, herbs (thyme through parsley), and enough hot Beef Stock to cover meat. Cover and cook on high 4 to 5 hours, until meat is very tender but not dry.

5. Discard herbs; serve ribs, juice, and vegetables over your favorite mashed potato recipe or, better yet, Chivey Potato Puree. Finish with fleur de sel or truffle salt, as desired.

RED WINE–POACHED TENDERLOIN WITH TARRAGON SPAETZLE

SERVES 4

Clearly no one in his right mind would make this recipe — poached beef what? But if you, like me, are not in your right mind, this recipe is a must-have in your repertoire. Poaching is a fantastic method for cooking an otherwise wimpy cut of meat, imparting a ton of flavor while sacrificing nothing in the way of texture.

TARRAGON SPAETZLE

½ cup milk
1 egg
½ teaspoon salt
¼ teaspoon freshly grated nutmeg
1½ cups flour
1 tablespoon chopped tarragon
1 tablespoon canola oil

Spaetzle dough

1. Mix together milk and egg in a small bowl.

2. Stir together salt, nutmeg, flour, and tarragon in a large bowl. Make a well in the dry ingredients and, using a whisk and then a spatula or wooden spoon, stir in milk mixture until just combined: do not overmix.

3. Cover and let rest 30 minutes. Meanwhile, prepare Red Wine Poaching Liquid (p. 125).

4. Bring 4 quarts of salted water to a boil.

5. Slice dough with a sharp, smooth knife on a dampened wooden board into small noodles, about 3 inches long. Working quickly so that spaetzle will cook evenly, scrape noodles into boiling water.

6. Boil vigorously until spaetzle float on water's surface. Using a slotted spoon, remove spaetzle from water, rinse under cold tap water, and toss with canola oil.

(recipe continues)

Red Wine–Poached Tenderloin with Tarragon Spaetzle

RED WINE POACHING LIQUID

1 teaspoon olive oil

2 carrots, peeled and cut into 1-inch pieces

2 onions, peeled and cut into 1-inch pieces

2 ribs celery, cut into 1-inch pieces

3 cloves garlic, smashed

1 teaspoon black peppercorns

3 cups red wine (merlot)

2 sprigs thyme

1. Heat a large (4-quart) saucepan over high heat 3 minutes. Add first 6 ingredients (oil through peppercorns); turn heat to low and sweat 10 to 15 minutes.

2. Add wine and thyme; turn heat to high and bring to a boil. Reduce heat and simmer 10 minutes. Remove from heat and cool to room temperature, then strain, discarding solids. Set aside.

TO POACH BEEF TENDERLOIN:

4 (6-ounce) fillets beef tenderloin

¼ teaspoon salt

¼ teaspoon freshly ground black pepper

4 tablespoons butter

1 teaspoon lemon juice

1. Bring red wine poaching liquid to a simmer in a small (1-quart) saucepan. Season beef fillets with salt and pepper. Add meat to poaching liquid (if liquid does not cover beef entirely, add red wine to cover). Keeping liquid to just below a simmer, around 150°F, cook 15 minutes; turn beef and cook an additional 15 minutes.

2. Remove beef from poaching liquid and set aside on a plate. Strain poaching liquid into a wide sauté pan over high heat and reduce quickly to 1 cup.

3. Reduce heat to medium and whisk in butter and lemon juice. If sauce is thick, add a teaspoon of water. Remove from heat and allow to rest. Slice reserved fillets in half crosswise.

(recipe continues)

To finish:
1 tablespoon canola oil
¼ teaspoon salt
Freshly ground black pepper
¼ teaspoon fleur de sel

1. Warm a large sauté pan over high heat. Add canola oil and heat to smoking point. Add spaetzle and cook over high heat, stirring frequently, until golden brown, about 3 minutes.

2. Divide spaetzle among 4 plates, add poached beef slices, season with pepper and fleur de sel, and drizzle with sauce. Serve.

I think about New York City less often than you'd expect. I've been back only a couple of times. It was where I earned my bones, where I began to understand what I was doing and why I was doing it. But it was also where I began to long for a home. I was lucky: the kind and gentle hands of fate ferried me through the kitchens of some of the great masters of our generation.

By the time I left New York, I had even found a partner, someone willing to take turns driving the getaway car. In 2002, we packed up our new kid and moved to Minneapolis. It was the most courageous move of my life, with my mentors warning me that if I left New York, my career would become meaningless. Somehow I knew that for me the move would close a door on noise and hysteria. It did so almost immediately. It was as if I had entered a quiet room; peacefulness descended. I began to understand the narrative of the choices I had made, and the silence allowed me the space to try to connect with other people.

I ate some of the great meals of my life in New York, but I had some bad ones, too. Meals that people lost their heads over, wrote reviews hyping them beyond compare. I believe the axiom that if you can make it in New York, you can make it anywhere may be just the opposite in food. If you could make great food in, say, Wisconsin Dells — if you could connect with not just the choir but with the guy slouching in the back row, if you could create excitement there — you would be an absolute food genius.

PORK BALLS AND TOMATO– WHEAT BERRY STEW

SERVES 4

Yep, the family loves this one too, despite — to quote the eight-year-old — the "weird" grain. Start with the wheat berries and be sure to cook them until tender.

FOR PORK BALLS:
½ teaspoon anise seed
1 teaspoon fennel seed
⅛ teaspoon red pepper flakes
½ teaspoon black peppercorns
3 whole cloves
1 pound ground pork
1 egg
1 teaspoon salt
2 tablespoons canola oil

1. Toast the dry spices (anise through cloves) in a medium sauté pan on high heat; remove from heat and finely grind mixture in a spice grinder.

2. Combine pork, ground spices, egg, and salt in a medium bowl. Mix together by hand, divide into 16 portions, and roll into balls.

3. Add canola oil to a large sauté pan over medium heat and cook pork balls until done, about 18 minutes, turning to brown on all sides. Remove from pan and set aside. Reserve pan for making the stew.

TOMATO–WHEAT BERRY STEW
1 cup uncooked wheat berries
½ cup Tomato Fondue (p. 167)
5 slices Tomato Confit (p. 168), chopped
½ cup water
1 teaspoon salt

1. Cook wheat berries according to package instructions, at least an hour. Drain and set aside.

2. Place sauté pan from pork balls over medium-high heat; add Tomato Fondue, Tomato Confit, wheat berries, water, and salt and bring to a simmer. Return pork balls to pan. Simmer to reduce liquid almost completely. Serve in bowls as a winter lunch entrée.

CURRIED GOAT WITH SPINACH AND RADISHES

Serves 4–6

No, I don't tell my kids their plates are filled with goat. They love it, and they still don't know. Sorry guys. Love, Dad.

For curried goat:

2 pounds goat meat, cut into 2-inch pieces

2 teaspoons salt

1½ tablespoons black pepper

1 tablespoon canola oil

8 cloves garlic, thinly sliced

4 to 5 cups Brown Chicken Stock (p. 162)

1 teaspoon turmeric

1 teaspoon Curry Powder (p. 155)

1 medium russet potato, peeled and chopped

1. Season goat with salt and pepper. Heat a large sauté pan over high heat 4 minutes. Add oil to pan, swirl to coat, and add seasoned goat. Sear meat until dark brown, turning to cook on all sides, about 10 minutes. Remove from heat.

2. Place meat in a slow cooker; add garlic, Brown Chicken Stock, and turmeric and stir to combine. Cover and cook on low 8 hours.

3. Refrigerate goat in the braising liquid at least 8 hours or overnight.

4. Defat braising liquid while cold; discard fat. Remove bones and fat from meat. Stir together meat, braising liquid, Curry Powder, and potato in a large saucepan and simmer on low about 45 minutes.

For spinach:

1 (5-ounce) bag prewashed baby spinach

½ cup radishes cut into julienne strips

1 teaspoon cornstarch

¼ teaspoon salt

3 tablespoons butter

1. Toss spinach, radishes, cornstarch, and salt together in a large bowl.

2. Heat a large sauté pan over high heat to nearly smoking. Add butter; melt and allow to brown. Add spinach mixture and cook and stir about 1½ minutes. The spinach juice will be absorbed, and the leaves will remain nice and plump.

TO FINISH:
Spread spinach across a platter and spoon on the stew, heaping it in the center. Serve family style.

SPICE-RUBBED AND GRILLED FLANK STEAK WITH SWEETBREADS SALAD

SERVES 4

FOR SWEETBREADS:
1 to 1¼ pounds sweetbreads
½ medium onion
1 carrot, peeled and halved lengthwise
1 rib celery, scrubbed clean and halved lengthwise
10 black peppercorns
4 sprigs thyme
1 bay leaf

1. Place all ingredients in a large saucepan and cover with about 4 cups water; simmer on low heat 3 hours.

2. Remove sweetbreads from saucepan; discard liquid and vegetables.

3. Break sweetbreads into small pieces, following the natural seam and discarding any sinew and fat. Set aside.

(recipe continues)

FOR STEAK:

1 teaspoon cardamom

½ teaspoon black peppercorns

¾ teaspoon salt

1 pound flank steak, trimmed of fat and sinew

2 tablespoons canola oil

1. Preheat grill to high. Toast cardamom and peppercorns in a small sauté pan on high heat; remove from heat and finely grind in a spice grinder. Add salt to spices and evenly rub mixture on both sides of steak.

2. Pound steak to about ¾-inch thickness using a meat mallet. Place steak on a plate and cover with oil.

3. Cook steak on a hot grill, about 4 minutes each side. Remove from grill and let rest 6 minutes. Slice at an angle into ¼-inch slices.

FOR SALAD:

1 star anise

3 whole cloves

½ teaspoon black peppercorns

Pinch cayenne pepper

1 (½-inch) slice candied ginger, finely minced

2 tablespoons canola oil

¼ cup flour

1 teaspoon salt, divided

1 bunch upland cress or watercress

½ radicchio, stem removed, cut into ¼-inch julienne strips

2 Belgium endives, cut lengthwise into ¼-inch julienne strips

4 green onions, thinly sliced

3 tablespoons Mustard Vinaigrette (p. 150), plus additional for steak, if desired

1. Toast star anise, cloves, and peppercorns in a small sauté pan on high heat; remove from heat and finely grind in a spice grinder. Add cayenne and ginger to spice blend; set aside.

2. Add oil to a large sauté pan and heat to smoking point. Toss the sweetbreads in flour and cook about 2 minutes, stirring to prevent sticking. Stir in ½ teaspoon salt and the spice mix; cook until brown, crisp, and heated through, about 2 minutes.

3. Remove sweetbreads from pan and toss with remaining ingredients (cress through Mustard Vinaigrette, including ½ teaspoon salt). Serve salad alongside steak, passing additional vinaigrette if desired.

Just a few short months ago, I would have told you there is nothing more important than salt: the mastery of cooking flows from a basic understanding of how to coax flavor from food, and an adequate amount of salt is central to the process. But when I started to cook these recipes at home, for my family, I noticed I used less salt, cutting back by a pinch here and there and relying more heavily on the ingredients to marry well and to allow their natural salinity to come through.

Pay close attention when salt is added to a recipe: oftentimes, it extracts moisture to result in more pronounced flavor, which means you need not use as much.

Salt is the only rock we eat, an essential mineral in our diet. Professional cooks view it mostly as a benign ingredient. In the business, we add salt the way photo editors might manipulate a supermodel's image: who could it possibly hurt? And anyway, "they" know we use loads of salt.

Too much salt can be a bad thing — you can say that about anything, I suppose. Cooking at home seems to have inspired in me a different feeling about salt: it's a necessary evil that should be used not just for its own sake but to produce real flavor. When you think about adding salt, consider this: will that salt catch up on your palate? By the time you have eaten a portion of whatever size, will you be thinking, "Wow, that was salty"? Unless, of course, you're trying to attract deer. Then, by all means, the saltier the better.

CRISPY TOFU AND BLACK BEAN SAUCE

Serves 4

Find fermented black beans at Asian grocery stores.

BLACK BEAN SAUCE
1 tablespoon canola oil
2 inches fresh ginger, grated
1 clove garlic, minced
¼ cup water
¼ cup soy sauce
½ cup liquid from Pickled Shiitake Mushrooms (p. 159)
¼ cup sugar
¾ teaspoon cornstarch
½ cup fermented black beans, rinsed, drained, and patted dry

(recipe continues)

Crispy Tofu and Black Bean Sauce

1. Heat sauté pan over medium-high heat. Add oil, ginger, and garlic; cook and stir about 12 seconds.

2. Add remaining ingredients (water through beans) and bring to a boil. Reduce by half, about 6 minutes. Remove from heat. Strain sauce, discarding solids, and set aside liquid; keep warm.

FOR TOFU:
1 pound soft tofu
1 teaspoon salt
4 sheets phyllo, sliced thin or shredded
2 tablespoons canola oil

1. Cut tofu into 4 slices lengthwise. Season slices evenly with salt. Moisten tofu slices slightly and wrap in sliced or shredded phyllo, pressing gently to adhere.

2. Heat a medium sauté pan over medium-low heat, add canola oil, and place phyllo-covered tofu in pan. Cook until browned, about 2 minutes, and then flip tofu and continue browning, 2 minutes more. Remove from pan, drain on paper towels, and slice diagonally.

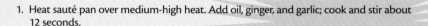

TO FINISH:
½ English cucumber, peeled, halved lengthwise, seeded, and sliced on the bias ¼ inch thick
3 Pickled Shiitake Mushrooms, thinly sliced, plus 2 tablespoons pickling liquid (p. 159)
2 tablespoons butter
⅛ teaspoon red pepper flakes

1. Stir together cucumber, shiitakes, and pickling liquid in a medium saucepan over high heat; bring to a boil. Reduce heat to medium and add butter and red pepper flakes, tossing to combine.

2. Divide vegetables among 4 plates, spoon over warm black bean sauce, and top with 2 pieces of crispy tofu. Serve.

DESSERTS

CHEESE PRESENTATION

SERVES 4

On break in a Paris kitchen, a coworker unwrapped a block of Pont l'Évêque cheese and ate it, casual as can be, as if it were a chocolate bar. Oh, the French.

I don't know about you, but I like a little somethin'-somethin' with my cheese, usually some toasted baguette slices (the toaster oven: one of the great inventions of humankind) or a small salad. This presentation is my favorite, one I have forced on my friends for years. Psst: it's all in the quality of the oil.

1 Belgian endive, outer leaves discarded, cut into ¼-inch julienne strips
½ cup finely chopped pineapple
½ tablespoon lemon juice
1 tablespoon extra-virgin olive oil
1 tablespoon sliced chives
¼ teaspoon fleur de sel
About ⅛ teaspoon freshly ground black pepper
3 to 4 ounces cheese per person: I like a variety — aged Cheddar, blue, and sheep or goat
1 baguette, sliced any way you like

Place Belgian endive, pineapple, lemon juice, olive oil, and chives in medium bowl; toss to combine. Add fleur de sel and freshly ground black pepper, toss again, and serve alongside cheese and baguette.

Cheese Presentation

CARROT CAKE WITH PINEAPPLE AND CARDAMOM

SERVES AT LEAST 12

I'm a big fan of carrot cake — and a bigger fan of cream-cheese frosting. Inspired by my mother-in-law's recipe, this version is even better than hers.

FOR CAKE:

2 cups flour

2 teaspoons baking powder

1½ teaspoons baking soda

1 teaspoon salt

1½ teaspoons ground cardamom

1½ cups oil

2 cups sugar

4 eggs, lightly beaten

2 cups freshly grated carrots

Carrot Cake with Pineapple and Cardamom

½ cup Pineapple Topping (p. 158)
½ cup chopped hazelnuts

1. Preheat oven to 350°F. Prepare two 8-inch round layer cake pans with cooking spray and line bottom of each pan with parchment paper; spray parchment paper.

2. Sift together flour, baking powder, baking soda, salt, and cardamom in a medium bowl. Set aside.

3. Combine oil, sugar, and eggs in bowl of standing mixer fitted with whisk attachment and mix briefly. Add dry ingredients and mix well, about 1 minute; add remaining ingredients (carrots through hazelnuts) and mix about an additional minute on medium speed.

4. Divide batter evenly between prepared pans; bake 30 minutes, until a wooden pick inserted near the center comes out clean.

5. Set cakes in pans on cooling racks about 5 minutes; remove cakes from pans and cool completely before frosting.

To frost cake:
With serrated knife and sawing motion, slice each cake round horizontally into two layers. (If you, like me, can't resist: munch on one layer while assembling the other three into the final cake.) Place one cake layer onto a cardboard round and spread a dollop of Cream-cheese Frosting on top from the middle to the edges, leaving sides exposed. Repeat with remaining layers, leaving the final golden layer exposed. Slice and serve.

BANANA-NUTELLA NAPOLEONS

SERVES 4

For phyllo crisps:
4 sheets phyllo, thawed
Clarified Butter (p. 166), melted
½ cup powdered sugar, divided

1. Preheat oven to 375°F. Cover workspace with plastic wrap.

2. Lay flat the first layer of phyllo dough; brush with Clarified Butter. Sift about 2 tablespoons

---

CREAM-CHEESE FROSTING

8 tablespoons (1 stick) butter, softened

8 ounces cream cheese, softened

2 cups powdered sugar

2 teaspoons pure vanilla extract

Combine all ingredients in bowl of standing mixer fitted with paddle attachment; blend on low to bring ingredients together, then on medium speed until smooth, about 8 minutes.

powdered sugar over entire surface of dough. Place the next phyllo atop the first layer, repeat butter and sugar steps, and follow with remaining sheets.

3. Transfer phyllo stack to parchment-covered cutting board. Using pizza wheel or large chef's knife, cut phyllo into 12 rectangles.

4. Transfer phyllo stack with parchment paper to baking sheet. Top phyllo with another piece of parchment and place another baking sheet snugly on top: the baking sheets and parchment now sandwich the phyllo.

5. Place trays in oven 10 minutes. Remove from oven and immediately pull off top tray and parchment; the crisps should be golden brown. Set aside to cool.

Banana-Nutella Napoleons

FOR NUTELLA FILLING:
¼ cup Nutella
3 tablespoons heavy cream

Stir together Nutella and cream and warm over double boiler, about 3 to 4 minutes, until smooth.

PRESENTATION:
2 to 4 bananas, thinly sliced and spread evenly on
    parchment paper
About ¼ cup sugar
1 cup heavy cream, whipped to soft peaks

1. Sprinkle bananas with sugar and, using a small hand torch or the oven's broiler, caramelize sugar.

2. Spread 1½ teaspoons Nutella filling on phyllo crisp and top with about 4 slices banana. Repeat. Add final layer of phyllo crisp and finish with 4 slices banana.

3. Repeat assembly steps for 3 more napoleons. Serve with a dollop of whipped cream.

I rounded the corner from the dish pit into the kitchen at Le Bernardin, and there at my station stood a young woman. I froze in my tracks, unable to muster strength to move another step. I was instantly and completely smitten. She wore her culinary school uniform, all pressed and straight, side towel at the ready. On her head, a tall hat. Her beautiful face was beaming with excitement.

She'd been assigned to help me for a little while before service started. I set her up with some Beldis lemons to clean, demonstrating the technique. I sought to strike up a conversation at several points but didn't get anywhere. Nothing, nada, no reaction. Undeterred, I pressed ahead, but every one of my canned lines seemed to set me further back, to resonate less and less.

Soon Eric called me into his office and handed me a stack of cards related to an important cause of his; I was to distribute them to each of the cooks. On my rounds, I attempted to hand one to this young lady. She simply said, "No, thanks."

"You can't say no. Just take it and put it in your knives and throw it away if you don't like it."

"Hardly," she said. "I would venture a guess that you didn't even look at what you're handing out. You're just doing what you're told. You don't know what that organization is and does."

"You're right," I said dumbly.

"Well, I'm not much of a follower, so take that to someone who is." She turned and walked away.

She didn't accept the job, instead choosing to travel to the West Coast to work with Ludo Lefebvre at L'Orangerie. When she moved back to New York, we bumped into each other from time to time at various cook-type get-togethers. Then later, under Jean-Georges, I put in a couple of months at Mercer Kitchen, where she also worked. We spent some time together, but the boss-underling dynamic did not do much to sway her affections in my direction. I grew tired of her constant scorn yet sensed that in her heart of hearts she kind of liked me. I was moved up to Midtown but had occasion to see her again when the crews from a few of JG's places got together downtown to celebrate New Year's 2001. I asked her to dance; she complied, ignoring me the entire time.

When the dance ended, we made our way back to our cocktails, and in a moment of utter madness I placed my open hand on her exposed midriff and whispered in her ear, "Let's go to my place and make this New Year's Eve amazing." She brushed my hand away, took a step back, looked me up and down, and said, "Finally, you've grown some balls. No, I won't go home with you tonight, but you can call me and take me on a date."

I did manage to sneak a kiss from her that night. Within months we had decided to get married and have a family. Is this a story of perseverance? I doubt it, but it does explain why these days I know that all the cute lines and subterfuge amount to nothing when compared to actually taking chances and living life to the fullest.

PINK PEPPERCORN ICE CREAM

MAKES ABOUT 1½ QUARTS

My sweetheart loves her ice cream. I think her happiest place on earth is cuddled up in a corner of the couch with her family around her and a big-ass bowl of ice cream on her knees. This recipe brings together Heidi's fantastic ice creams and my weird fascination with pink peppercorns. Serve it with South Minneapolis Peanut Butter Brownies (p. 148) or chocolate sauce and sprinkles. Wedge yourself into the couch and enjoy.

1 teaspoon pink peppercorns
1 cup sugar
8 egg yolks
2 cups whole milk
2 cups heavy cream

1. Grind peppercorns with mortar and pestle; stir together with sugar in a small bowl. Set aside. Place yolks in a separate, large bowl. Set aside.

2. Bring milk and cream to a boil in a medium saucepan over medium heat. Meanwhile, set a medium bowl inside a larger bowl of ice water and set out a fine-mesh strainer.

3. Whisk together peppercorn sugar and yolks. Temper yolk mixture by gradually whisking in the milk mixture.

4. Return ice cream base to saucepan and cook, over medium-high heat, stirring constantly with a wooden spoon, about 5 minutes, until mixture is thick enough to coat the spoon.

5. Immediately pour mixture through fine-mesh strainer into bowl set in ice bath. Discard solids. Refrigerate ice cream base until completely cool, even overnight, to develop flavors.

6. Freeze mixture in an ice cream maker according to manufacturer's instructions. Serve.

ALMOND AND MASCARPONE BUNDT CAKE

SERVES 12–14

FOR CAKE:

3 cups all-purpose flour

½ cup almond flour

1¼ teaspoons coarse salt

¼ teaspoon baking soda

1 cup (2 sticks) butter at room temperature

3 cups granulated sugar

6 eggs at room temperature

2 teaspoons lemon zest (from about 3 lemons; reserve juice for glaze)

1 tablespoon lemon juice

1 cup mascarpone

Almond and Mascarpone Bundt Cake

FOR GLAZE:

⅓ cup freshly squeezed lemon juice

½ teaspoon Orange Powder (p. 155)

2 cups powdered sugar

Stir together all ingredients, adding a little water if the mixture seems thick, and drizzle over cooled cake. Slice and serve.

1. Preheat oven to 325°F. Prepare a 12-cup Bundt pan with butter and flour. Whisk together flours, salt, and baking soda.

2. Combine butter and sugar in bowl of standing mixer fitted with paddle attachment; beat on medium speed until pale and fluffy. Add eggs, 1 at a time, beating well after each addition. Beat in lemon zest and juice.

3. Turn mixer to high and beat until ingredients are smooth and well incorporated, a couple of minutes.

4. Reduce speed to low and add one-third of the combined dry ingredients, scraping the bowl as necessary. Add one-third of the mascarpone. Repeat twice more, alternating dry ingredients and mascarpone. Mix until well combined but not overworked.

5. Pour batter into prepared pan and bake until cake is golden brown and a wooden pick inserted near the center comes out clean, 1½ to 1¾ hours. Allow to cool in pan for about 10 minutes; then turn out on to wire rack. Cool at least 1 hour before adding Glaze.

CITRUS-DRENCHED CAKE WITH SABAYON

SERVES 4

Goofy name, *sabayon*, but a simple, tasteful dessert. Because it sounds exotic, most people probably assume it's complicated, but even if you've never believed me before, believe me now: it's easy. You can bake the cake and prepare the citrus the night before.

FOR CAKE:

1 cup cake flour

1 teaspoon baking powder

¼ teaspoon salt

3 eggs, separated

1 cup sugar

1 teaspoon vanilla extract

¼ cup milk

(recipe continues)

Citrus-drenched Cake with Sabayon

1. Preheat oven to 350°F. Prepare a 9-inch-square pan with butter and flour.

2. Sift together cake flour, baking powder, and salt onto a piece of parchment paper.

3. Place egg yolks in the bowl of a standing mixer fitted with whisk attachment and add sugar and vanilla. Mix at medium speed until fluffy, about 5 to 10 minutes.

4. Turn mixer to low and slowly add milk. Return to medium speed and add about one-third of the flour mixture, mixing until combined, about 1½ minutes. Repeat with remaining flour mixture in two more additions.

5. Beat egg whites to nearly stiff peaks in a medium mixing bowl. Gently fold whipped egg whites into batter using a rubber spatula.

6. Pour batter into prepared pan. Bake about 30 to 35 minutes, until top is light brown. Cool in pan on rack about 10 minutes; then invert and remove from pan. Let cool completely on rack. Slice for serving.

CITRUS AND JUICE MIXTURE
1 grapefruit
2 oranges
1 lime
1 lemon
2 tablespoons brown sugar

1. Slice off top edge of grapefruit to the juicy flesh; repeat on bottom edge so that fruit sits flat on cutting board. To remove both skin and pith, peel from top to bottom, placing knife at an angle on the inner edge of the skin and following the fruit's curve. Repeat on each side until the skin is completely removed.

2. Hold fruit above a medium bowl to catch juices. Slice along membrane line separating one segment and then down the other side, pushing knife at an angle underneath and then up to remove that segment. The fleshy part of the segment — called the *supreme* — comes out, leaving the membrane behind. Repeat on all sides, running the knife along the membranes.

3. Squeeze membranes over bowl to release juices; discard membranes. Repeat steps with oranges, lime, and lemon, placing all supremes in bowl with juices.

4. Stir in sugar and refrigerate until ready to use.

SABAYON

4 egg yolks
¼ cup sugar
¼ cup dessert wine
1 cup heavy cream

1. Fill a large (3-quart) saucepan halfway with water and bring to a boil. Reduce heat to low to maintain a gentle simmer. Prepare a large bowl of ice water.

2. In a medium heat-resistant bowl placed over — but not touching — simmering water, whisk egg yolks and sugar until pale and slightly thickened. Do not allow mixture to become too thick, or it will curdle.

3. Gradually pour in wine, whisking vigorously and constantly, until mixture nearly triples in volume and drops like a ribbon from the elevated whisk. Remove from heat.

4. Place bowl over ice-water bath and whisk until mixture cools.

5. In a medium bowl, whip cream to medium peaks; gently fold cream into sabayon base. Cover tightly with plastic wrap and refrigerate until ready to use.

TO FINISH:
Place a couple of cake slices on each of 4 plates. Spoon fruit and juice mixture evenly atop cake. Top with a big spoonful of sabayon. Finish with Mint Oil (p. 159), if desired, or shredded fresh mint leaves. Serve.

SOUTH MINNEAPOLIS PEANUT BUTTER BROWNIES

SERVES AT LEAST 16

These brownies have it all: they're thick, crispy, chewy, and lightning fast. My tip: make this simple preparation seem like a herculean effort, and then steal a little time for yourself.

1 cup (2 sticks) butter
4 ounces unsweetened chocolate, chopped
2 cups sugar
3 eggs, beaten
1 cup flour
2 teaspoons vanilla
½ cup chopped salted peanuts
½ cup peanut butter chips

1. Preheat oven to 350°F. Prepare a 9-inch-square pan with butter and flour.

2. In a medium (2-quart) saucepan over medium-low heat, melt butter and chocolate. Remove from heat.

3. Using a wooden spoon, stir in sugar, then eggs, then flour, then vanilla. Lastly and quickly fold in peanuts and then chips.

4. Pour batter into prepared pan and bake about 30 to 35 minutes; the brownies will be moist: a testing toothpick will show a few crumbs. Cool, cut, and serve.

CILANTRO PESTO

MAKES ABOUT 1 CUP

Don't be tempted to cut down this recipe: once the pesto's in the fridge, you'll find yourself using it on everything.

1 bunch cilantro leaves and stems, rinsed thoroughly in cold water
1 tablespoon toasted sesame oil
½ teaspoon Sriracha
⅛ teaspoon salt
1 tablespoon fish sauce
¼ cup cold water

1. Bring 2 quarts water to a hard boil and add 1 teaspoon salt. Blanch cilantro until tender, about 30 seconds. Remove from boiling water and rinse under cold tap water until cool, 10 seconds. Squeeze out excess water; roughly chop.

2. Place blanched and chopped cilantro in container of electric blender and add remaining ingredients (sesame oil through water). Cover and blend on high until smooth, about 1 minute. Refrigerate until ready to use.

MUSTARD VINAIGRETTE

MAKES ABOUT 2 CUPS

Keep this versatile vinaigrette on hand and use it to finish dishes ranging from grilled fish all the way to asparagus.

1 clove garlic, minced
1 teaspoon salt
2 tablespoons whole-grain mustard
1½ tablespoons red wine vinegar
¾ teaspoon freshly ground black pepper
½ cup extra-virgin olive oil
2 tablespoons warm water

Combine all ingredients and whisk by hand 3 minutes. Refrigerate until ready to use.

These days, it's harder and harder to go to the mall: the proliferation of great cooking stores conspiring to consume my paycheck is frightening. Equipment that once could be found only through professional sources is readily accessible. This availability has no doubt helped fuel an explosion in the variety and use of cooking gear. Consequently, kitchens have become the latest bastion for gadget collections. When I conquered my wife's kitchen, I agreed to maintain it in its original condition—meaning I wasn't permitted to fill it up with a bunch of new toys.

Here's what you need: A heavy cutting board that is easy to clean. A couple of sharp, low-maintenance knives: a paring knife and an 8-inch utility knife will get most jobs done. Heavy weave towels for picking things up: those oven gloves your mom had can be clunky and hard to maneuver. A fish spatula, a couple sizes of high-temp rubber spatulas, a few timers, and you're on your way.

When you're setting out to create food that will make people happy and that you will enjoy cooking, there's no need for any pretense. Think of it this way: in a different room (I suppose in the kitchen, too), a negligee might spice things up, but chances are the better it looks, the shorter the amount of time it will stay on, anyway. If a tool has a single use, avoid it, unless you enjoy dusting. Spend the dough you save on good ingredients.

CITRUS VINAIGRETTE

MAKES ABOUT 2 CUPS

A good mixture to have on hand, this extremely versatile dressing goes great with beets as well as lighter leafy greens like butter lettuce.

2 teaspoons coriander seed, toasted and ground
½ teaspoon hot Chinese mustard
1½ teaspoons orange zest
1 orange, juiced
1½ teaspoons lemon zest
½ lemon, juiced
2 teaspoons freshly grated ginger
¼ teaspoon cayenne pepper
1 tablespoon sugar
½ cup rice wine vinegar
1½ cups canola oil

Combine first 9 ingredients (ground coriander through sugar) in blender and process on high for about 1 minute. Add rice wine vinegar; blend on low 1 minute. With blender on low, slowly add canola oil until combined. Refrigerate until ready to use.

DIPPING SAUCE

MAKES ABOUT 2½ CUPS

Pair this sauce with Seared Salmon Spring Rolls (p. 14).

1 jalapeño pepper, sliced thin
1 clove garlic, sliced thin
6 tablespoons sugar
1½ cups water
3 tablespoons fresh lime juice
10 tablespoons fish sauce
¼ cup shredded carrot

Combine all ingredients in medium bowl and whisk until sugar is dissolved. Refrigerate until ready to use.

The award for the least-favorite meal my mom served was a chicken curry dish with raisins and rice.

As the youngest kid in the family, I learned early on to be wary of advice offered by my big brothers. Along the way one of them told me to avoid eating the raisins because they were actually flies, a specialty trait of Indian cuisine. "It really isn't the same without the flies," he said. It took me years to eat curry without cringing.

Not until I worked with Floyd Cardoz at Lespinasse did I begin to understand that *curry* means only a spice blend, a particular flavor profile typically named for the region from which it hails.

Turmeric is often included in curries, but I am not at all a fan of the spice, so this recipe doesn't call for any. Some say turmeric's health benefits are considerable, but something about the combination of flavors takes me right back to my parents' dining room table, my brother whispering in my ear, "watch out for the flies."

PS: You will find a couple of exceptions to this rule in the book, including the recipe for Curried Goat (p. 128). Turmeric and goat love each other, and one should never get in the way of a good love affair.

GARAM MASALA

MAKES ABOUT ¾ CUP

A nice blend to keep around the kitchen, Garam Masala is available in the spice aisle, but taking the time to create your own will add a unique touch to your cooking. Increase the anise by 2 teaspoons if you like licorice; drop the cloves by 10 for a winning midsummer combination.

½ cup mint leaves
10 teaspoons coriander seeds
5 teaspoons cumin seeds
5 teaspoons anise seeds
4 teaspoons cardamom pods
2 teaspoons ground cinnamon
25 whole cloves
1 pinch saffron

1. Rinse mint leaves and dab dry. Place leaves on parchment paper–lined baking sheet and set out to dry overnight. Crush mint leaves with mortar and pestle, yielding about a teaspoon of crushed mint.

2. Toast remaining ingredients (coriander through saffron, excluding mint) in a medium sauté pan on high heat until they begin to smoke and pop, about 4 minutes. Remove from heat.

3. Add mint to hot pan and stir quickly; pour out spice on plate to cool.

4. Process small batches of spice mixture with a spice grinder until ground into a powder. Store in airtight container for later use.

Curry Powder ingredients

CURRY POWDER

This spice mix is handy to have around the kitchen. Store in an airtight container out of direct sunlight up to 2 months.

30 cardamom pods
24 cloves
12 star anise
12 tablespoons coriander seeds
6 teaspoons cumin seeds
2 teaspoons fennel seeds
2 teaspoons fenugreek
3 teaspoons cayenne pepper

1. Toast first 7 spices (cardamom through fenugreek) in medium sauté pan on high heat until fragrant and beginning to smoke and pop, about 4 minutes. Remove from heat.

2. Add cayenne to hot pan and stir quickly; pour out spice on plate to cool.

3. Process small batches of spice mixture in a spice grinder until ground into a powder. Store in airtight container for later use.

ORANGE POWDER

MAKES 1 TEASPOON

For years I've been preaching that folks should keep this zesty add-in on hand. It frankly adds tons of flavor to even the simplest of dishes. Sprinkle a little on your morning toast with some Nutella spread. Yum!

3 oranges

Zest oranges with a microplane onto a parchment paper–lined baking sheet. Place zest in a cool area to dry for a day or two. Crush into fine powder using a mortar and pestle; store up to 3 months in an airtight container.

CHIP MIX

MAKES ABOUT ¾ CUP

Use to make Spiced Football Potato Chips (p. 14).

1 tablespoon plus 1 teaspoon black peppercorns
1¼ tablespoons fennel seed
4 tablespoons sugar
3 tablespoons kosher salt
2 teaspoons paprika
1 tablespoon onion powder
1 tablespoon garlic powder
1 teaspoon ground ginger
¼ teaspoon cayenne pepper

1. Toast peppercorns and fennel seeds in a sauté pan over high heat for 1 minute, until aromatic. Remove from heat, allow to cool, and process to a fine powder with a spice grinder.

2. Combine ground pepper and fennel with remaining ingredients (sugar through cayenne); mix well. Store mixture in airtight container away from direct sunlight up to 3 months.

POACHED SHRIMP

MAKES ABOUT 1 POUND

2 cups Shrimp Stock (p. 160)
1 pound large (26/30) shrimp, peeled and deveined

Bring Shrimp Stock to a simmer. Add shrimp, turn heat to medium-low, and baste shrimp with stock 3 minutes. A "C" shape is what you're looking for; "O" means overcooked. Remove shrimp from stock, set shrimp aside, and reserve stock for later use.

GRILLED SHRIMP

Serves 4–6

1 pound large (26/30) shrimp, peeled and deveined
1 tablespoon canola oil
1 teaspoon salt
¼ teaspoon freshly ground black pepper

Preheat grill to high. Toss shrimp in oil and season with salt and pepper. Place shrimp on hot grill; cook 2 minutes and then flip and cook an additional 2 minutes. Remove from heat. Serve immediately or refrigerate up to 1 day.

PICKLED SHALLOTS

Makes about 2 cups

This recipe is one that can hang out in the fridge for a while—an arrow in your quiver, so to speak. When the moment comes, use the liquid in a vinaigrette, replacing the vinegar in a 2:1 ratio with the canola oil, or in a beurre blanc for fish, especially Broiled Salmon (p. 89).

1 star anise
1 cinnamon stick
½ teaspoon red pepper flakes
1 tablespoon fennel seeds
2 tablespoons coriander seeds
½ bay leaf
1 cup sugar
1 cup white vinegar
5 shallots, thinly sliced

1. Toast the first 5 ingredients (star anise through coriander seed) in a medium sauté pan on high heat; remove from heat, add bay leaf, and finely grind the mixture in a spice grinder.

2. Place ground spice mixture, sugar, and vinegar in a medium saucepan; bring to a boil and simmer 3 minutes.

3. Place shallots in a separate medium saucepan and strain spice liquid over top. Discard solids. Bring the mixture to a boil and simmer 10 minutes. Remove from heat.

4. Allow mixture to cool. Refrigerate until ready to use.

PINEAPPLE TOPPING

Makes about 3 cups

If you're smart—and I know you are, since you bought this book—spoon this topping over Pink Peppercorn Ice Cream (p. 142) and South Minneapolis Peanut Butter Brownies (p. 148).

1 pineapple, peeled and cored
½ cup sugar
½ cup water
½ vanilla bean

1. Dice half of pineapple into ¼-inch squares; set aside. Roughly chop other half.

2. Place chopped pineapple into large saucepan with sugar and water and bring to a boil. Simmer 5 to 6 minutes, until cooked. Remove from heat.

3. Place cooked pineapple mixture in container of electric blender; cover and process until smooth, about 1 minute.

4. Return pineapple puree to saucepan; add vanilla bean and bring to a boil. Add reserved diced pineapple and simmer about 2 to 3 minutes. The sauce should be thick. Refrigerate until ready to use.

MINT OIL

MAKES ABOUT ⅓ CUP

I keep mint oil on hand to use in various dishes, from fruit salad to pastas. It beats the heck out of buying a bunch when you need only a little and then watching the leaves turn in the fridge.

1 cup loosely packed mint leaves, rinsed well under cold water
⅓ cup canola oil

1. Bring 3 quarts water and 1 tablespoon salt to a boil. Blanch mint leaves 5 seconds. Remove leaves and rinse under cold water until cool.

2. Squeeze leaves dry and place in container of electric blender; add canola oil. Cover and process 1 minute, scrape down sides, and process 1 additional minute. Refrigerate oil up to 1 week.

PICKLED SHIITAKE MUSHROOMS

MAKES ABOUT 1 CUP

1 star anise
1 cinnamon stick
½ teaspoon red pepper flakes
1 tablespoon fennel seed
2 tablespoons coriander seed
½ bay leaf
1 cup sugar
1 cup white vinegar
8 ounces fresh shiitake mushrooms, stems removed

1. Toast first 5 ingredients (star anise through coriander) in a small sauté pan over medium heat until fragrant, about 4 minutes.

2. Stir together spice mixture, bay leaf, sugar, and vinegar in a medium saucepan over medium heat; bring to a boil, reduce heat, and simmer 3 minutes. Remove from heat.

3. Place shiitake caps in a large saucepan and cover with pickle liquid. Bring to a boil; remove from heat. Allow mixture to cool; refrigerate mushrooms in liquid up to 2 weeks.

FUMET

MAKES ABOUT 2 QUARTS

2 pounds fish trim and bones (preferably white, flaky fish like halibut)
1½ tablespoons salt
15 cups cold water, divided
¾ cup dry white wine
1 teaspoon white peppercorns
15 parsley sprigs

1. Add fish bones and salt to 8 cups cold water and soak 15 minutes. Rinse fish and discard water.

2. Stir together remaining 7 cups water, wine, peppercorns, and parsley sprigs with fish bones in stockpot. Bring to a simmer; continue to simmer on low 30 to 40 minutes.

3. Strain mixture, discarding solids, and cool broth. Refrigerate until ready to use, 3 to 4 days, or freeze up to 3 months.

SHRIMP STOCK

MAKES ABOUT 2 CUPS

1 tablespoon canola oil
6 ounces shrimp shells (from about 2 pounds shrimp)
⅛ teaspoon salt
4 tablespoons tomato paste
4 cups cold water

1. Heat oil to smoking point in a large sauté pan. Add shells and stir vigorously 1 minute. Evenly distribute shells in pan, add salt, and cook and stir 5 minutes, until shells are light golden brown.

2. Remove from heat. Add tomato paste, stirring to combine. Add water, return to heat, and bring to a boil. Reduce heat and simmer 30 minutes.

3. Pour stock through a fine-mesh strainer, pressing shells with the back of a spoon to extract as much liquid as possible. Discard shells; refrigerate stock.

BLOND CHICKEN STOCK

MAKES ABOUT 2 QUARTS

I usually freeze this stock in 2- to 3-cup increments, just the right size for most recipes.

2½ pounds chicken wings and bones
2 tablespoons salt
20 cups water, divided
1 clove garlic, peeled and halved crosswise
1 teaspoon black peppercorns
½ leek, white only, scrubbed clean and finely chopped

1. Cut chicken into small pieces; rinse well. Place chicken in stockpot, add salt and 10 cups water, and soak 15 minutes. Drain chicken and rinse under cold running water.

2. Add chicken, remaining 10 cups water, and remaining ingredients (garlic through leek) to stockpot; turn heat to high and bring to a simmer. Reduce heat to maintain simmer; cook 2 hours.

3. Strain stock, discarding solids. Refrigerate stock, or freeze up to 3 months.

Most baffling to me about eating in some restaurants is that members of the staff don't taste the food they serve. It's incredibly odd, but it seems the norm.

As a result, it's difficult to criticize folks for eating at chain restaurants: at least the food has some taste to it. Oh, sure, I have my bones to pick about loading grotesque portions of food full of salt, fat, sugar, and chemical additives that people don't suspect are there. But all too often independents get caught up in the excitement, in the day to day, and forget to eat the food they are serving. Probably they assume that since they tasted it once and they prepared it the very same way they don't need to taste it again. This common mistake is repeated from the weaker restaurants almost all the way up the ladder.

Never trust a skinny chef. True, some of the fat ones just can't stop eating—they'll eat anything and like it. But you will save countless eye rolls if only you taste the food before putting it on a plate. Taste it as close to the temperature at which you will serve it, but for the love of God, taste it.

BROWN CHICKEN STOCK

MAKES ABOUT 3 CUPS

¼ cup canola oil
2½ pounds chicken wings and bones
½ teaspoon salt
½ leek, white only, scrubbed clean and finely chopped
1 teaspoon whole black peppercorns
6 cups water, divided
1 clove garlic, halved

1. Heat roasting pan in oven 10 minutes at 400°F. Add canola oil to roasting pan; heat 2 minutes. Add chicken wings and bones and salt. Roast in oven about 1 hour, stirring every 10 to 15 minutes. Add leek and peppercorns to pan; roast 15 minutes.

2. Transfer roasted chicken, leek, and peppercorns to an 8-quart stockpot. Deglaze hot roasting pan with 2 cups water, scraping up all of the brown bits. Add deglazing liquid, remaining 4 cups water, and garlic to stockpot.

3. Bring pot to a simmer on high heat; reduce heat and simmer 3½ hours.

4. Strain stock, discarding solids. Refrigerate stock, or freeze up to 3 months.

BEEF STOCK

MAKES ABOUT 4 CUPS

After freezing the stock in square or rectangular containers, I transfer the "blocks" into labeled plastic freezer bags, which take up a little less space.

1 tablespoon canola oil
4 pounds beef neck bones
½ teaspoon salt
1 onion, finely chopped
8 cups cold water, divided
½ tablespoon whole black peppercorns
1 clove garlic, peeled and halved

1. Heat roasting pan in oven 10 minutes at 500°F. Warm canola oil in hot roasting pan. Add neck bones and sprinkle with salt. Roast bones in oven 1½ hours, turning halfway through. Add onion and roast an additional 30 minutes, stirring occasionally.

2. Transfer contents of roasting pan to an 8-quart stockpot. Deglaze hot roasting pan with 2 cups water, scraping up all of the brown bits. Add deglazing liquid, remaining 6 cups water, peppercorns, and garlic to stockpot. Bring pot to a simmer on high heat; reduce heat and simmer 3½ hours.

3. Strain stock, discarding solids. Refrigerate stock, or freeze up to 3 months.

Beef bones for stock

MUSSEL STOCK

MAKES 1¼ CUPS

This is a secret recipe: don't tell anyone.

1 pound mussels
¼ cup white wine

1. Rinse mussels under cold running water 10 minutes. Place mussels and wine in a stockpot and cover with a tight-fitting lid.

2. Cook over high heat 5 minutes, then reduce heat to low and cook an additional 5 minutes. Remove from heat and let stand, covered, 10 minutes.

3. Pour mussels and liquid into a colander set inside a bowl. Let mussels drain about 5 minutes to extract as much stock as possible. Discard mussels (when cooked right, they will have yielded their moisture and won't be much fun to eat, so give them the heave-ho). Refrigerate stock until ready to use, 3 to 4 days, or freeze up to 3 months.

LOBSTER STOCK

1 (½-pound) live lobster
1½ teaspoons salt, divided
2 tablespoons canola oil
2 tablespoons butter
1 cup brandy
1 (6-ounce) can tomato paste

1. Bring 6 cups water and 1 teaspoon salt to a boil in a pot large enough to hold the claws.

2. Using a sharp chef's knife, cut straight down on lobster's head and through eyes to kill it. Twist off tail and place in an oven-safe bowl. Twist off claws and arms.

3. Remove bands from claws using a paring knife and place claws and arms in boiling water, cooking until thumb separates easily from claw, about 8 minutes. Remove from water and allow to cool. Pour remaining boiling water over tail to submerge; let stand 3 minutes, remove from water, and allow to cool. Separate shell from meat. Reserve meat for future use: refrigerate 1 to 2 days or freeze up to 2 months.

4. Remove outer shell from inner shell connected to legs. Remove brain from outer shell and discard; place outer shell in the bowl of a standing mixer fitted with paddle attachment.

5. Scrape lungs off inner shell using a paring knife; discard lungs and add inner shell and legs to the bowl. Add reserved tail and claw shells.

6. Cover mixer with plastic wrap to keep shells inside bowl. Turn mixer to low to make a mushy mess of lobster shells and guts, mixing for about 15 minutes.

7. Heat a large (2- to 3-quart) saucepan over high heat; add canola oil and heat until nearly smoking. Add lobster shells and guts and cook, stirring occasionally, for 2 minutes. Add ½ teaspoon salt and butter, which will foam and brown. When foam subsides, turn off heat and add brandy to deglaze pan. Scrape the browned bits from the bottom, turn heat to high, and carefully ignite brandy with a long match or a barbecue lighter.

8. Once the flambé has subsided, add tomato paste and sweat about 1½ minutes, stirring. Add 4 cups water and bring to a boil; reduce heat and simmer 22 minutes.

9. Pour through a fine-mesh strainer, pressing solids to extract as much liquid as possible. Refrigerate until ready to use, 3 to 4 days, or freeze up to 3 months.

CRÈME FRAÎCHE

MAKES ABOUT 1½ CUPS

1 cup heavy cream
½ cup buttermilk

Stir together cream and buttermilk in a glass jar and cover. Let stand at room temperature 24 hours, until thick. Store, refrigerated, up to 2 weeks.

CLARIFIED BUTTER (GHEE)

MAKES ¾ CUP

1 cup (2 sticks) butter, cut into small cubes

Melt butter slowly in a saucepan on low heat over a couple of hours. Skim and discard froth that rises to the surface. Strain the clear melted butter into an airtight container. Store, refrigerated, up to 5 days.

GARLIC CONFIT

MAKES 2 CUPS

This garnish is very handy, but garlic in oil can grow deadly bacteria, so eat within a couple of days. To use, simply pop the cloves out of their shells, remove the root end, and either smash or leave whole as you prefer.

1 head garlic, excess paper removed, broken into unpeeled cloves
2 cups canola oil
⅛ teaspoon salt

Place ingredients in a small saucepan and bring to a slight simmer. Continue to simmer until garlic is soft, about 15 minutes. Cool; refrigerate in a glass jar.

TOMATO FONDUE

MAKES ABOUT 1½ TO 1¾ CUPS

I freely admit I can't stand fresh tomatoes. Early on in the game I had an allergic reaction, and ever since I don't trust them. Once a year when they are perfectly in season, I will have some sliced with a little salt — but that's the limit. Cooked tomatoes are a different story, however: those I love. This is my all-time favorite tomato thing to have in the fridge. I'll put it on anything — except fresh tomatoes, that is.

2 pounds tomatoes, cored
4 cloves garlic, thinly sliced
¼ cup extra-virgin olive oil
½ teaspoon salt

1. Bring a large pot of water to a rapid boil. Prepare a large bowl of ice water.

2. Drop 2 to 3 tomatoes into boiling water for 8 seconds. Immediately remove them from the water using a slotted spoon and place into the ice-water bath. After about a minute, remove tomatoes from ice water and peel using a paring knife. Repeat with remaining tomatoes.

3. Halve tomatoes and squeeze out seeds into a strainer set in a bowl to collect juice. Discard seeds; set aside tomato juice and tomato halves.

4. In a large (4-quart) saucepan, sweat garlic in olive oil over low heat until fragrant. Add tomato halves, salt, and juice. Bring mixture to a simmer and cook over low heat about 3 hours, until nearly entirely reduced. Remove from heat. Store refrigerated up to 1 week, or freeze up to 3 months.

TOMATO CONFIT

MAKES ABOUT 30 PIECES/1 CUP

8 Roma tomatoes, scored and cored, blanched and peeled (see instructions on p. 167)
½ cup sugar
½ cup water
¼ cup extra-virgin olive oil
½ tablespoon chopped fresh thyme
1 teaspoon fleur de sel
¼ teaspoon black pepper

1. Preheat oven to 200°F. Slice tomatoes into ½-inch rounds. Dissolve sugar and water in a small bowl to create a simple syrup. Pour olive oil onto plate.

2. Dip each tomato slice into simple syrup, coating both sides. Remove with fork, dip into olive oil to coat both sides, and place on a parchment paper–lined baking sheet. Evenly top each piece with chopped thyme, fleur de sel, and pepper.

3. Bake 3 hours with oven door open 2 inches. Flip tomato slices and bake an additional 3 hours, watching carefully toward the end to prevent burning. Store in the refrigerator, and use as you would a sun-dried tomato, in sauces or salads.

MAYONNAISE

Makes about 1¼ cups

1 (pasteurized) egg yolk
½ teaspoon salt
½ teaspoon dry mustard
⅛ teaspoon sugar
⅛ teaspoon turmeric
2 teaspoons freshly squeezed lemon juice
1 tablespoon white wine vinegar
1 cup canola oil

1. Whisk together egg yolk and dry ingredients (salt through turmeric) in a glass bowl.

2. Stir together lemon juice and vinegar in a separate bowl. Thoroughly whisk half of lemon juice mixture into yolk mixture.

3. Whisking briskly, add oil a few drops at a time, then increase to a constant stream. After half the oil is incorporated, add remaining lemon juice mixture.

4. Continue whisking, adding remaining oil until incorporated. Refrigerate until ready to use, up to 1 week.

BEURRE FONDUE

Makes about ½ cup

1½ tablespoons water
8 tablespoons (1 stick) butter, cut in small cubes

Bring water to a simmer in a small saucepan. Gradually whisk in butter to creamy consistency, constantly watching heat to maintain a bare simmer; if emulsion becomes too hot, it will break down. Remove from heat and keep warm until using in a recipe like Vegetarian "Bolognese" (p. 64).

Something wonderful happened at Heidi's. It seems so obvious as to be painful, but looking back on it now, I had gone into it completely unaware of how the restaurant's size would teach us to focus on what matters most.

The space itself was tiny, a little over 1,100 square feet, in which we had the small entrance, host stand, kitchen, service area, bathroom, and forty-five to fifty seats. There was not much room at all. The kitchen was also tiny, offering barely the space to open the oven doors, about enough room to lay out seven to ten plates at a time.

I had worked in small kitchens, but nothing like this. I suppose it wasn't just the size of the space but the size of my ambitions that made for an interesting scenario. I could not create dishes that had fifty ingredients—I just plain didn't have the room to maneuver. As it was, not a nook or cranny didn't have something on it or in it or around it.

There was no choice but to scale back my ambitions, and, as is almost always the case when one reassesses and minimizes, I was reminded of just what is essential. When situations, tools, ingredients are boiled down to their basic elements, sometimes wonderful things happen. Looking back, I seemed so rich in my cramped space. I hope as time goes on and as a new Heidi's opens, I can hold on to these moments in my home kitchen and remind myself that the simple version is almost always the best.

EPILOGUE

As I gave these pages one final look, imagining myself as a reader, I began to wonder where the author's head was when he choose the stories and selected the recipes. Of a lifetime spent in the kitchen, the elements collected here seemingly represent some low-hanging fruit.

So please allow me yet another moment of your time. Just as Ricky demanded of Lucy, I've "got some 'splainin' to do!"

In some sort of Rumsfeldian way, not only do we go to war with the army we have, we write with the intellect we have. For the sake of brevity, I'll operate under some basic assumptions going forward. That you have chosen to read this epilogue implies you have enjoyed the "pudding" of this cookbook. Perhaps you are still reading because you find my writing compelling. No, that is the least-likely scenario; the mostly likely is that you wondered what the heck the chap was on about the whole time.

It's been only a few months since the fire that destroyed Heidi's Minneapolis. We had been open for two and a half years, much of which was spent trying, meta-phorically, to tread water and keep up with the demand for reservations. The Saturday before the fire had been our record night. We were realizing our dreams of owning a successful restaurant — and then in what felt like a moment, we watched it disappear. You will have to forgive me if I seem to be overdramatizing the signifi-cance of this event: every day, total bummer things happen to people that are far worse. But the fire did happen. I wish at times that it had not, that it was not a part of our history.

Time for us has passed slowly. Often Heidi or I mention to each other in amazement that it's been only a short while since such a shocking thing happened, since our world was turned upside-down. I sat the other day in a design meeting to create a new restaurant — a new Heidi's — feeling downright sorry for myself. I didn't let it show, but across the table I could see the hurt on Heidi's face, too, and the sadness for what has been lost.

We lose things all our lives: people we love dearly, jobs we like and don't, friends — everything. Somehow in these moments of pain and suffering and sadness we are lost ourselves, and so completely found.

I could not set out to write this book today. The immediacy of the emotions, my fervent link to the food we had created — it's as if a close friend had died and I had the time to sit down and write about him for a few weeks. This book is of the place and time in which it was written. It is a thin slice, a snippet of three months after my world changed unexpectedly. But I needed to tell these stories, and in the context of a career, the low-hanging fruit is also the most ripe, the most worthy of eating and sharing. What didn't disappear that day was who we are, how we are who we are. These stories represent the remains, the important stuff you realize you hadn't much thought about when things were hunky-dory, the people we meet who change our lives — sometimes we don't even know how much until years later, when we arrive at a fork in the road.

On the Fourth of July, standing over the huge welded steel cooker we had rented for the day, I mentioned to a cousin that I had never done this before — roasted a whole pig. She laughed and said, "Now you know how the rest of us feel when we go to cook things." In that moment I knew why I wanted to write a cookbook in the first place.

Everyone who puts together a cookbook, I venture to guess, hopes that people will feel a level of comfort to try the recipes and perfect them to their taste. I hope that when folks set out to cook from this book they will hear my voice guiding them, inspiring confidence to prepare a meal or use a technique that is wholly new to them.

The real reason behind this book, the bottom line, the raison d'être is nothing more than this: the idea of not sharing recipes or food or ideas or meals with others is freaking unbearable. We cook — at least I do — to satisfy more than just a fascination with chemistry and the alchemy of emotions and memories that flavors and scents conjure up. We — I — cook to provide sustenance to people. Often I'm feeding total strangers, but it's a two-way street: their appreciation, their participation in the food we create is the nourishment of my soul.

Thank you for taking this trip with me. I can't wait to see what the next ride will be. I hope that you'll join me for it — and that you'll find a way to share your passions with the world, no matter how rough the seas sometimes can be.

INDEX

THANKS

It's good to give thanks.

I have been blessed through the years to have worked with some tremendously talented people. They have informed, entertained, and enlightened. They weren't just famous chefs: they were also dishwashers, line cooks, guests, farmers, and friends. Fellow cooks, fellow foodies, and folks that just plumb like to eat.

In particular I would like to thank Frankie, Kyle, Liz, Kate, and the team at Heidi's for always being game to try anything. And the folks at Borealis Books, including Shannon and Pam, who loved our ideas and who courageously signed us up and cheered me on through the process of writing my first book.

I am the chef and person I am as a result of working — and sweating — with these people. This book is the sum total of the treasure that is our fellowship.

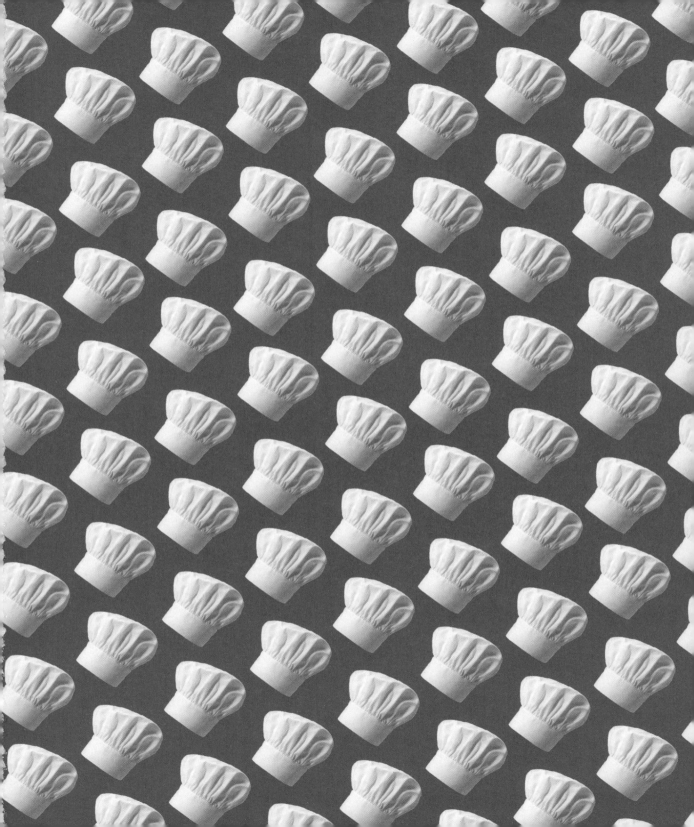

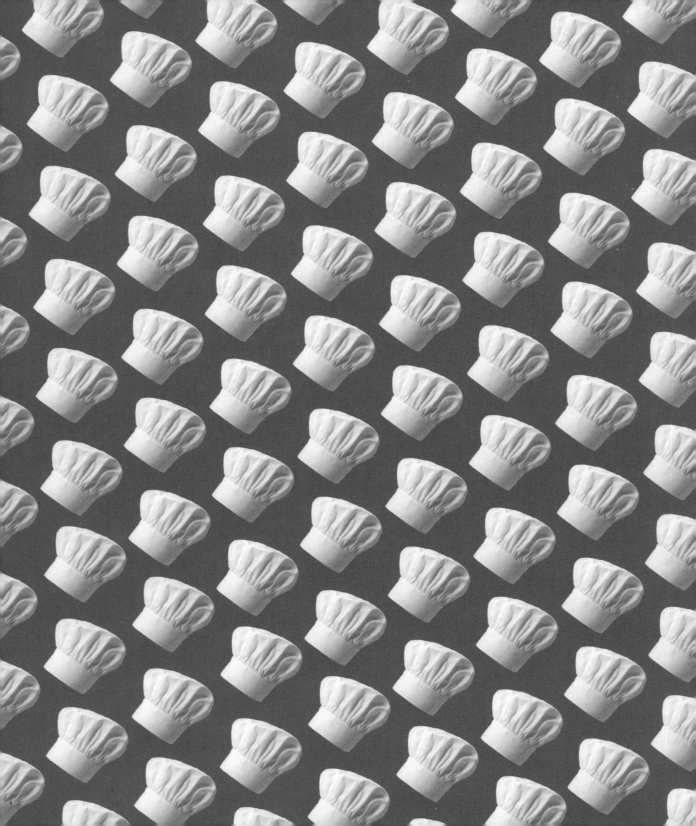